CLIFTONSTRENGTHS
FOR STUDENTS

Your **strengths** journey begins here

FROM GALLUP

GALLUP PRESS
The Gallup Building
901 F Street, NW
Washington, D.C. 20004

Library of Congress Control Number: 2017931422

ISBN: 978-1-59562-125-2

First Printing: 2017
10 9

Printed in Canada by Friesens

TO COLLEGE STUDENTS
EVERYWHERE WHO WANT TO
APPLY THEIR STRENGTHS TO
CHANGE THE WORLD

Don Clifton
(1924-2003)

Inventor of CliftonStrengths® and recognized as the
Father of Strengths-Based Psychology by an American
Psychological Association Presidential Commendation

Table of Contents

Part One: Your College, Your Strengths, Your Journey 1

Part Two: CliftonStrengths Themes in Action 47

Achiever 51

Activator 55

Adaptability 59

Analytical 65

Arranger 71

Belief 75

Command 79

Communication 85

Competition 91

Connectedness 95

Consistency 99

Context 103

Deliberative 107

Developer 113

Discipline 117

Empathy 121

Focus 127

Futuristic 131

Harmony 137

Ideation 141

Includer 147

Individualization... 151

Input 155

Intellection.. 159

Learner.. 163

Maximizer 167

Positivity 173

Relator 179

Responsibility... 183

Restorative 187

Self-Assurance 191

Significance 195

Strategic... 199

Woo.. 203

References.. **209**

The History of CliftonStrengths **213**

About Gallup **219**

Acknowledgements **223**

Part One:

Your College, Your Strengths, Your Journey

• • •

Kristen put a lot of thought into where she was going to go to college — and what she was going to do once she got there.

She made 10 visits to seven schools. For each one, she made a spreadsheet filled with all the classes she would take. She finally made a decision and enrolled at a large Midwestern college where her brother was the only other person she knew.

Her priorities were: make friends, have a meaningful experience and really learn how to "go with the flow."

Now, going with the flow never had been among Kristen's strong suits. In fact, she felt like she had to change the "controlling," "unspontaneous" parts of herself when she got to college. She saw those attributes as weaknesses.

During freshman orientation, Kristen completed the CliftonStrengths assessment and found out that her top five themes were Discipline, Individualization, Harmony, Focus and Significance. A week later, she met with Mike, one of the professors on campus, who was also a strengths coach. He told her that the "controlling," "unspontaneous" parts of her were not weaknesses; they were strengths.

"Professor Mike became a real mentor for me," Kristen says. "He truly helped me understand where I was at my best and how I could get involved and make an impact on campus."

According to Professor Mike, trying to become laid back was not only unnatural for Kristen, but it would make it harder for her to succeed.

"I started to see my Discipline strength as a net gain rather than a net loss," Kristen says. "Coming out of that coaching meeting, I knew I wanted to get involved on campus, and I knew I had something to give. So I applied to be an orientation leader as a freshman."

During the orientation leader interview, Kristen talked about how important it is for her to have routines, to plan ahead, to be orderly and to create predictability for others. She talked about her strengths, but she didn't use CliftonStrengths terminology. She wanted to show that she had the talents for the role, but she didn't expect the interviewer to speak the same "strengths language."

"Then the interviewer stopped me, leaned over the table and said, 'Do you have Discipline? Me too!' She told me she was one hard nut to crack and that she never smiles, but she smiled that day when she realized what we had in common," Kristen says. "That's what CliftonStrengths does — it creates a shared language that breaks down barriers and brings people together."

Kristen got the orientation leader position. She joined a sorority, made friends and did well in her classes. Bit by bit, she became involved and engaged on campus.

Eventually, Kristen was elected president of her sorority. She used her Harmony talents — her natural ability to bring differing factions together — to lead her sorority sisters through some struggles they were experiencing. Later, she applied her leadership skills and talents to a campus-wide strengths rollout for all incoming students. She also served as a student strengths coach for her peers.

"I was proud of my unique talents and jumped into teams, knowing that I had something special to bring to the table. It was OK that I wasn't as 'go with the flow' as other people," she says. "In fact, as time went on, I learned how to partner with people who could complement me and who made me more confident in my own strengths."

By the time the intense, once uncertain freshman graduated from college, she was extremely involved on campus. She served as an orientation and enrollment leader and as the dean's student assistant at the college of human ecology. She was a hospice volunteer and president of her sorority. She even won an award from the dean of student life for being one of the top 16 graduating seniors for improving student life. And, she graduated summa cum laude.

Today she is a nonprofit executive who leads her organization using a strengths-based approach.

Now, imagine if Kristen had rejected who she really is — forever feeling self-conscious about her "controlling," "unspontaneous" personality — rather than embracing her true self. How might her life have turned out differently?

Kristen learned something radically important: When students not only know their strengths — but more importantly, apply them — the effect on their lives is transformational. And after graduation, they will have a big head start. Gallup has found that people who use their strengths every day are six times more likely to be engaged in their work and three times more likely to say they have an excellent quality of life.

As Kristen discovered, college is a chance to start fresh. Regardless of your background, age or reputation in high school, you begin with a clean slate — which is really liberating — and a chance to learn and grow in ways that will amaze you.

Like Kristen, you get to write your own story.

So what do you want your story to be? Begin your journey with the end in mind. What will your legacy be when you leave college? You have already begun to chart this journey, and you'll have a better perspective if you understand when and where you're at your best: your strengths.

Strengths begin with talents, those patterns in your thoughts, feelings and behaviors that are most consistent and reliable and that make you unique. When you add skills and knowledge to those talents, you can develop them into strengths. As a student, you get the chance every day to search for patterns in your actions, to learn from them, and to use them to understand your life experiences now and in the future. That knowledge is vital because you'll find unlimited potential in your strengths.

But building a great life and a thriving college experience requires something more: making a real commitment to putting your strengths into action. Knowing and using your strengths has an impact on every aspect of your college experience. But first, **you must know yourself and see yourself as unique, gifted and motivated.** This begins with identifying your talents so you can see where you are at your very best.

CLIFTONSTRENGTHS

To get you started, this book includes an access code to take the CliftonStrengths assessment. This unique code is in the packet in the back of the book. After you complete the assessment, you'll receive a report that lists your top five themes of talent (your "Signature Themes") and access to resources to help you better understand your unique talents.

Knowing what your leading themes are is the first step to turning them into strengths. After you learn your top five themes, look them up in the second half of this book. For each theme, you will find several action items, which include questions, ideas and suggestions you can use to develop your talents in each theme and start turning them into strengths.

Understanding how to use your unique strengths will make your college journey — and the rest of your life — happier, more fulfilled and more successful. That's the point of developing your strengths. It may be the most useful thing you'll ever learn.

Strengths-Based Philosophy

You are different from the people sitting around you. In fact, you are so unique that the chances of you having the same top five talent themes as someone else are about 1 in 275,000. The odds of having the same top five themes in the *exact same order* are 1 in 33 million.

Because of your talent themes, your experiences and your environment, you look at life in a unique way. Many people think they need to be exactly like someone else, whether that's a celebrity, some other towering figure of success, or somebody they know and admire. But trying to be someone else doesn't work. Becoming more of who you *already are* is the key to your success.

Who you are is a gift given to you at birth — you are born with a set of talents that nobody else has. Turning your unique talents into strengths requires skills, knowledge, conscious effort and deliberate action — all applied to the things that matter to you. While success means different things to different people, everyone achieves their version of success by fully developing and applying their strengths. Nearly 70 years of research has proven it.

In the early 1950s, Don Clifton, a popular psychology instructor and researcher at the University of Nebraska, started thinking about all the ways the field of psychology had to describe what is *wrong* with people — medically, psychologically and socially — and the very few ways it had to identify what is *right* with people.

Clifton began researching why some people become great at what they do and others don't. For one project with ROTC students in the mid-1950s, he looked closely at the common factors of successful people. The study kept expanding, and in 1998, Clifton, who was then chairman of Gallup, sought to invent a common language and talent themes to describe what people do well.

So Gallup researchers mined their database, which contained more than 100,000 talent-based interviews at the time, and looked for patterns. They examined specific questions that Gallup had used in studies of successful executives, salespeople, customer service representatives, teachers, doctors, lawyers, students, nurses and people in several other fields.

Through this process, Clifton and Gallup researchers established the 34 themes of talent. Researchers then developed the first version of the CliftonStrengths assessment to measure these distinct talents. As of this writing, more than 16 million people have taken the assessment. And the American Psychological Association officially gave Clifton a presidential commendation as the Father of Strengths Psychology.

What CliftonStrengths actually measures is talent, not strength. The assessment is called "CliftonStrengths" instead of "CliftonTalent" because the ultimate goal is to build a true strength, and talent is the primary component in the strengths formula.

That's why the CliftonStrengths assessment does not include any questions about your formal education, degrees or résumé. Nor does it ask about your skills — whether you can speak fluent French, build a website or fix a transmission. While knowledge and skills are important, along with regular practice, they are most helpful when they serve as amplifiers for your natural talents.

Though people do change over time and personalities evolve, scientists have discovered that core personality traits are relatively stable throughout adulthood, as are people's passions and interests. And research suggests that the roots of personality might be visible at a young age. A 23-year longitudinal study of 1,000 children living in New Zealand revealed that children's observed personality at age 3 shows remarkable similarity to their reported personality traits at age 26. That's why CliftonStrengths measures talent — talents don't really change much.

Knowledge, skills and practice — along with talent — are vital parts of the strengths equation. You will likely develop skills and knowledge through your experiences in school, in work settings and in hands-on practice. When you supplement your talents with your knowledge and skills to the point that you can consistently provide near-perfect performance in a given activity, you have developed a strength. And by applying and even further refining your strengths, you move closer to fulfilling your natural potential as an individual.

Building your talents into strengths requires practice and hard work, much like building physical strengths. For example, if you have a natural talent for running, the more miles you put in, the faster you'll get. People with less talent for running can put in those same miles, but their speed won't improve as much as yours will. A 1950s research project on speed-reading with 10th-graders found that practicing boosted everyone's words-per-minute reading rate. But those who started out reading fast (300 words a minute at the beginning of the study) made more gains (2,900 words a minute at the end of the study) than everybody else did. All the kids improved, but practice helped the kids who had talent for reading improve the most.

Knowledge and practice will help you move from good to great in your areas of talent. But remember, there's a limit to how much you can do. Everyone is talented, but no one is talented at everything. If you spend your life trying to be good at everything, you will never be great at anything. Many colleges — and society as a whole — encourage you to be well-rounded, thinking that if you work hard enough, you can master anything. But you can't.

Trying to become well-rounded breeds mediocrity. You can master the things you're naturally good at, but if you're working on something that is outside your areas of talent, you'll become, at best, OK at it. Trying to be well-rounded at the expense of being great is a waste of your time and talents. In fact, of the leaders Gallup has studied, those who strive to be competent in the most areas become the least effective leaders overall.

Just like knowing what your talents are, you need to identify your areas of weakness so you know where to concentrate your energy and where not to. Gallup describes a weakness as anything that gets in the way of your success. Simply being aware of your areas of weakness can help you avoid obstacles.

Once you can acknowledge, for example, that you're not great at managing details, you can figure out how to make managing details less of a problem. The first question to ask yourself is whether you need to operate in your area of weakness at all. If you can just avoid doing detail-oriented work, by all means, stop.

Of course, most people don't have the luxury of ignoring necessary tasks just because they aren't naturally good at them. When you have to attend to details, you might need to establish support systems — checklists, reminder apps — to manage your weakness and keep you on track.

Another strategy is to partner with someone who has talent in the areas you don't. For example, being innately good at making people feel included (which is a talent in the Includer theme) is a lesser talent for Tyler. Tyler will rush to assemble a group without considering everyone who might need to be involved, and sometimes, he leaves people out. So he has learned to find partners who naturally include others. They help him think about people he would have overlooked — and who might ultimately make a group stronger.

It's also in your best interest to become aware of any blind spots that your talents cause. For example, Susan has strong Command talents, and she may not realize the damage left in her wake as she pushes to get things done each day. Or take Caspian, who has dominant Consistency talents. He might focus so much on keeping the steps uniform and become fixated on the process that he ignores the overall goal. So while Susan's and Caspian's talents push them to achieve amazing things, their blind spots can sometimes narrow their perspective.

The 34 CliftonStrengths themes describe a great deal of the variation in human talent and provide a common language, but they do not capture every nuance of unique personalities. The fine points of talents and how they are expressed vary a great deal from person to person. For example, you and your friends may all have Learner among your top five themes, but each of you might express that theme differently. One of you may learn from voracious reading, while another learns from doing and yet another learns by talking with others. No instrument can measure every subtlety of every talent in every situation, but CliftonStrengths offers the best and most concise explanation of talents and themes.

And millions have taken the first step on their strengths journey. As mentioned earlier, more than 16 million people have taken the CliftonStrengths assessment, and Gallup has helped thousands of organizations all over the world become strengths-based. A big part of being a strengths-based company is matching employees' strengths to their roles. The more people can align their strengths with their work, the more engaged they will be in their careers. The same goes for college. The more you align your strengths with your college experiences, the more you can engage with your campus and your studies.

But to be engaged, you have to be involved. Joining clubs, making friends, and seeking mentors and professors who care about you while staying financially healthy and applying what you learn in the classroom are all part of a great college experience. To have success in all of these areas, you need to understand what makes you unique and what makes you great — your strengths. When you apply your strengths to make your campus and college better, those experiences will change you.

THE BIG SIX

To better understand what makes a college experience great for students like you, in 2014, Gallup and Purdue University began measuring the impact of the experiences students have in college on their later lives. This study of more than 30,000 U.S. college graduates, called the Gallup-Purdue Index, assesses alumni's perceptions of their undergraduate experiences and how those experiences relate to their engagement and job quality later in life.

The Gallup-Purdue Index shows that there are six key collegiate experiences — the "big six" — that are critical to being engaged at work. Among college graduates who had all six of these experiences, 65%, on average, were engaged. Of the alumni who didn't have any of the big six experiences, only 25% were engaged.

The Big Six Experiences

1. Had at least one professor who made you excited about learning

2. Had professors who cared about you as a person

3. Had a mentor who encouraged you to pursue your goals and dreams

4. Worked on a project that took a semester or more to complete

5. Had an internship or job that allowed you to apply what you were learning in the classroom

6. Were extremely active in extracurricular activities and organizations

The Big Six: Mentorships and Relationships

You may have noticed that the first three big six experiences focus on relationships. Yet, people often underestimate the importance of their closest relationships and social connections and how they affect campus engagement, academic success and their sense of belonging. The people you know and the people you love have a great deal of influence on how you experience your life. So those you are closest to can influence whether or not you thrive on campus.

Experience 1	Had at least one professor who made you excited about learning

When alumni look back on their college experience, they say their relationships mattered most. But the people who had the biggest impact on their lives weren't their friends (though they were important). The people who had the biggest impact were their professors. The first of the big six experiences is having a professor who makes you excited to learn. That professor doesn't have to teach a class related to your major. The person is more important than the subject. The crucial thing is to have a professor who makes you look forward to class, who makes time fly during class and who gives you so much to think about when you leave class that learning seems more like fun than work. You may decide that a career in the subject the professor teaches isn't for you, but the experience of being excited to learn from a great teacher is important.

> **Experience 2** — Had professors who cared about you as a person

Do you have a professor whose teaching style inspires your learning — someone who gives you valuable feedback and who you are truly getting to know? Making a connection with one or more of your professors can be a powerful experience that has enduring benefits. It's rare for professors to chase down students to get to know them better, so you might have to seek them out and kick-start a deeper relationship. The long-term effects might be more far-reaching than you think. An expert who cares about you as a person can help you find innovative ways to use your strengths in a subject area you're passionate about.

> **Experience 3** — Had a mentor who encouraged you to pursue your goals and dreams

A mentor might be a professor, a member of the administration or maybe your boss. Usually, a mentor is someone who has a wider perspective and more life experience than you do. The best mentors give you good advice and inspire you to further *your* hopes for *your* life. They provide individual and personal guidance that aligns with your strengths and plans. Their direction and affirmation are invaluable when you're starting out in life.

Ultimately, what the first three big six experiences reveal is that alumni who have thriving careers and lives had important relationships that began in college: mentors, someone who encouraged their dreams, and at least one professor who cared about them and made them excited to learn. So as you think about your college experience, remember that the people you create relationships with now may influence the rest of your life.

Scientists are discovering just how much relationships shape expectations, desires and goals. Emotions can spread quickly from one person to the next. According to a Harvard study, your odds of being happy increase by 15% if a direct connection in your social network is happy. And if a friend of your direct connection is happy, the odds of you being happy increase by 10% — even if you don't know or interact with this secondhand connection. So your friends' friends have an impact on you and vice versa. The same holds true with your professors, mentors and others in your social network.

Having close friendships and mentorships in general is good for your health too. Relationships can serve as a buffer during tough times, which can improve your cardiovascular functioning and decrease your stress levels — especially helpful during finals. On the other hand, people with very few social ties have nearly twice the risk of dying from heart disease and are twice as likely to catch colds, even though they are less likely to have the exposure to germs that comes from frequent social contact.

Some students, however, might think they should focus on school and nothing else. After all, the classroom is the epicenter of the campus experience — where they will ultimately succeed or fail. But your sense of engagement on campus depends on more than grades alone. It's important to spend time with people and not just bury your head in your studies. When you think back on your college years, what you will remember most will be the people — the teachers, mentors and friends you made along the way.

So go see a band on Friday night with your roommate. Ask your favorite professor to have a cup of coffee with you. Seek out a mentor and ask how you — given your strengths — can accomplish your goals.

And keep socializing and networking. The sheer amount of time you spend interacting with others makes a difference. Studies show that when people have almost no social time, their chances of having a good day or a bad day are 50/50. However, each hour of social time quickly decreases their odds of having a bad day. The data suggest that you need at least six hours of social time to have a great day. Those six hours include all your social interactions: talking with classmates, coworkers and friends; reading texts and sending emails; and even chatting with the barista who makes your mocha.

So when you think about your campus involvement and connections, remember that spending time with others and having at least one close friendship is essential to your ability to thrive. And each additional friendship can contribute even more.

Gallup has found that people who have at least three or four very close friendships are healthier and are more engaged in their jobs. The absence of any close friendships can lead to boredom, loneliness and depression. That's one reason some college students want to transfer. They think they will find better friendships at a new school. The reality is that regardless of where you are, you need to be able to forge meaningful relationships using your unique set of talents and strengths.

Arun is a college sophomore who intentionally keeps his list of good friends short. He prefers authenticity over quantity in friendships. He attributes that to his Relator theme, which makes him inclined to keep a small social circle made up of people who truly know him. Arun says he has always been this way. "But I didn't realize it was a pattern until I saw my roommate's and my top five themes posted on our door when we were freshmen," he says. "It said the Relator theme pulls me toward people I already know and that I really like being around close friends more than just acquaintances. I guess I thought everyone was like that — why *wouldn't* you prefer a tight group of really good friends? But seeing how different my roommate's list was, well, it made me wonder."

The next day at Arun's freshman orientation, he attended a coaching session on his CliftonStrengths assessment results just like Kristen did at her campus. "That's where I realized that my pattern is really a talent and that it kind of guides my choices," Arun says. "Then, a professor for a class I'd signed up for said she was basing a group project on strengths. I got to thinking about how my Signature Themes were going to play out in a group." During a breakout session, Arun talked to his academic adviser and learned more about how he could use his strengths to be successful at school.

"Then the university president stood up and talked about his Individualization strength and how he saw each of us as unique. He told us to forge our own paths with an understanding of what's best in us and to use it in everything we do," Arun says. "School, work, relationships, all of it. Pretty soon, I realized that just being aware of my themes makes me more deliberate, I guess you'd call it. I'm just more intentional and aware about my relationships, and they've gotten better ever since."

Today, Arun says that his own Individualization theme causes him to see his closest relationships like the spokes on a bike — they keep his life balanced. His father always asks him good questions and motivates him. His girlfriend gets him out of the house more than he would on his own. His tight-knit group of fraternity brothers helps one another through financial problems, relationship issues, and health and academic challenges. His favorite professor works through his questions and concerns with him, and his mentor helps him think about his future and how what he is learning will apply to his career.

"One thing I noticed is that I rely on a network of people because no one person can do everything," he says. "And I don't necessarily get the same thing I give in my relationships." That's not unusual: More than 80% of the people Gallup studied report that they contribute something very different than they receive from their closest friendship. As Arun found, the key to great relationships is focusing on what each friend, mentor and professor uniquely contributes, instead of expecting one person to do it all.

The Big Six: Academics

> **Experience 4** Worked on a project that took a semester or more to complete

Think back to when you were in grade school sitting through a class in which you had very little interest. Perhaps your eyes were fixed on the clock or you stared blankly into space. You probably remember waiting anxiously for the bell to ring so you could get up from your desk and move on to whatever was next.

Now compare that to a class you loved. The teacher was caring and engaging and taught with passion. The style and subject perfectly aligned with your strengths and who you are. You loved everything you were learning, and you didn't even notice the time because it flew by. You even looked forward to going to class.

What was the class? How did you feel when you were in the class?

It's important to identify that class and that feeling because that's when you were at your best. Psychologist Mihaly Csikszentmihalyi coined the term "flow" to describe the phenomenon that occurs when you enjoy a task so much that you lose track of time.

You experience flow when you feel challenged and stretched, but more than equal to a task. Think of flow as being "in the zone." Everything falls into place. You don't exactly know how you did it, but you excelled, and you were deeply satisfied. People who have developed strengths and who are in environments that allow their talents to flourish are far more likely to experience flow.

Think again about that grade school class or another time when you experienced flow — when your strengths were so deeply aligned with what you were doing that time disappeared and you couldn't wait to tell your friends about what you learned and thought about. Having a passion for what you're studying and being able to apply your strengths in the classroom are vital to your engagement on campus.

When you register for classes, ask yourself two questions:

1. *Will I be able to apply my talents in this class?*

2. *Will I be able to apply my strengths to a long-term project?*

If you don't know the answer to either of these questions, get more information about the class. If you answer "no" to both questions, ask yourself why you are enrolling in the class in the first place. Applying your talents and spending a semester or more in experiential learning can make a huge difference in your future engagement with the school.

Remember that you see the world through the lens of your unique talents. For example, if you have Relator as one of your top five themes, search for long-term projects that have small group discussions. If you have Responsibility, make sure you are clear on the expectations and outcomes of the project. If you have Woo or Communication, find assignments where you can speak and process verbally. Academic programs that align with your talents will allow you to be your best in the classroom and when you need to commit to ongoing projects. They will also set you up for success in your career.

However, because every major has a list of course requirements, you will almost certainly have to take some classes and work on some projects you don't like. But applying your talents and relying on others can help you get through them, and you might even learn something from the experience.

Take Anson and his dreaded syllogistic logic class, for example.

"I'm majoring in fine arts, but my adviser said she wouldn't sign off on my course list unless I signed up for syllogistic logic," Anson says. "I thought that was super dumb. I've gotten by my whole life without knowing what syllogistic logic is. Why should I waste time and money to learn now?" But because it was a requirement, Anson took the class, and he hated it as much as he figured he would. So he relied on talents to get through it.

Anson has a lot of Focus, which he used to make himself concentrate on the work he found boring and repetitive and to gauge his progress. And he did make progress — a little each day.

The other talent he used wasn't even his own. "I met a girl at the first-year orientation who had Positivity as her No. 1 theme, and when I saw she was in my syllogistic logic class, I made sure to sit next to her every day. I figured her positive outlook might rub off on me, and she did make the class a lot less unpleasant," he says.

It wasn't until the class was over that Anson realized it helped him mitigate a weakness: writing. Anson doesn't enjoy writing and says he would put off writing a paper forever if he could. But syllogistic logic teaches people to think in sequence — one thing leads inevitably to the next.

"I have to take a bunch of literature classes, which I also don't want to take because that means writing about a million papers," Anson says. "A blank screen makes my blood run cold — where do you even start? But with syllogistic logic, you start with something small that you already understand, and you build on it, one thing at a time." Anson realized that he could use that same process with writing. He starts with something he understands, and then he thinks through what he read to build on the original idea. "As much as I dislike writing, it's so much easier if you know how to think it through," he says.

While Anson learned the value of applying his strengths to something he wasn't good at and didn't want to do, he also stumbled across another powerful resource: *other people's strengths*. The student with Positivity in her top five helped Anson get through the syllogistic logic class just by being herself. Gallup calls that a complementary partnership — finding someone with dominant talents that you lack. No one has all the talents needed to tackle every problem. So finding a complementary partner is a great way to get the most out of everyone's talents. When it comes to long-term projects or classes, knowing the strengths of others is vital to your learning and the project's outcome.

Here's an example of a group of students who would have benefited from understanding one another's strengths. Michael, Neeraj and Tim are friends who are working on a long-term class project together. When they meet, Michael and Neeraj immediately jump into task mode, while Tim starts brainstorming about the project. Michael doesn't mind. After all, they need ideas, and he doesn't pay much attention to what either of his partners is doing anyway. But Neeraj often gets upset. He usually thinks Tim is wasting time, and he gets frustrated by what he perceives as Tim's lack of focus. And Tim thinks Neeraj is bossy and trying to control the project.

Now suppose that their professor had taken the time to explain how talents affect group dynamics for the project. Further, suppose the professor had designed some strengths-based group exercises that would have helped students get to know one another and figure out how they could best use their talents to work together.

With those insights in mind, Neeraj and Michael would have known to listen intently to Tim's brainstorming because he has Ideation and Maximizer in his top five, and his new ideas could make the project better. Tim would have appreciated Neeraj's Responsibility and Focus talents to make sure the project gets done on time. And Michael would have used his Individualization talents to highlight and support both of his partners' unique contributions to bring excellence to the project.

And these are people who know and like each other. Appreciating others' perspectives and what they contribute is far more difficult among strangers. And just about everybody on campus is a stranger to you, at least for a while.

Understanding yourself and others — and where each of you is at your best — gives you the chance to truly grow, develop and succeed. A big part of enjoying college and succeeding in long-term group projects is simply being comfortable enough with who you are and what you have to offer that you can share yourself with other people.

The Big Six: Internships and Careers

> **Experience 5** Had an internship or job that allowed you to apply what you were learning in the classroom

Ever since you were a child, well-meaning people have been asking, "What do you want to be when you grow up?" The pressure to make the right career choice only intensifies as you head to college. Choosing a career is a daunting task, and you're not alone if you struggle with it. Some people avoid making a choice as long as possible. Others choose whatever job turns up or whatever career they think will make their parents happy.

For many years, Gallup has been asking employed adults, "Do you like what you do each day?" Given that adults employed full time in the U.S. report working an average of 47 hours per week, this might be the most basic yet important question to ask. Unfortunately, only 20% of people give a strong "yes" in response to this question. Only 13% of employees say they find their work meaningful, and a mere 20% think they're in jobs that use their talents.

You may not know the best career choice for you right now. However, an internship or job that allows you to apply what you are learning lets you explore a career so you can discover the things you might love about it as well as the things you might not. You get to decide what's best for you, and these opportunities can help you figure out what that is. What's more, alumni say that having a job or internship in college that allowed them to apply what they learned in the classroom played a part in their short-term and long-term success.

Isabella started college with a pre-med major. But during her junior year, after a semester-long internship at a hospital, she realized that while she loved biology, she just wasn't drawn to becoming a doctor. Her adviser suggested that she could have a fulfilling career in biological research. So after graduate school, Isabella got a great job in a research center.

Three years later, Isabella was asked to lead a team that would explore small research projects and dissertations that have an impact on a larger scale. With Significance, Learner and Individualization in her top five, Isabella discovered how much she enjoyed getting to know her team members as individuals, and she loved that they could achieve so much together.

Although laboratory work fascinated her, Isabella realized she had the talent for — and got the biggest rush from — leadership. So she went back to school, got an MBA and now runs a biotech research company. When she graduated from high school, she had no idea that any of the jobs she had after college even existed, but an internship and knowledge of her strengths gave her the perspective she needed to be successful.

The opportunity to choose your career, rather than taking whatever job you can get to pay the bills, is one of the reasons you are in school. But that doesn't mean you have to have your entire career path plotted on the first day of your freshman year. College gives you an outstanding opportunity to match your innate talents and strengths to your interests and apply them to hands-on experiences on campus.

The Big Six: Clubs and Organizations

Experience 6   Were extremely active in extracurricular activities and organizations

Every so often, you might see alumni on your campus gazing at the buildings, waiting patiently in the hallway to talk to elderly professors and spending a fortune on college sweatshirts at the campus store. If you ask them why, their eyes will light up, and they'll tell you how life-changing college was for them. Those alumni tend to have something in common — they were engaged and active on campus. That involvement created a profound sense of community, and it stayed with them.

That's why being involved and engaged in your college experience is so important. Graduates who say they were extremely active in extracurricular activities and organizations while attending college are nearly two times more likely to be engaged at work than their peers. When you participate, you can become part of a community with a common purpose, build networks and make a lasting impact on issues that matter to you.

There are likely dozens of clubs on campus that would give you the opportunity to develop your strengths, deepen your roots and boost your engagement. But be selective. Being heavily involved with a few meaningful groups has more of an impact on your campus engagement — and is better for your résumé — than joining countless organizations that don't interest you as much. Whether they are political, social, academic, religious, environmental, artistic, athletic or completely random, most organizations can probably really use your strengths. So join a club, run for office, get on a team or find the organization that fits you — you'll get as much out of participating as you put in.

Mauricio, a sophomore engineering student, grew up in Los Angeles and enrolled in a small college in Wisconsin. "People thought I was nuts, going to school so far from home where you can freeze to death eight months a year," Mauricio jokes. "But this school offered me a full ride, and when I visited, I loved that the school's colors and sports schedules were in every restaurant and coffee shop in town. I just felt safe and part of something bigger than myself. That and the scholarship — I couldn't pass it up."

But moving to Wisconsin was harder than he thought. "It was tough at first. People talk different here, they dress different and they don't do the things we do back home," he says. "Seriously, ice fishing?" When he got his CliftonStrengths assessment results during freshman orientation, he realized that none of his top five themes — Analytical, Ideation, Discipline, Responsibility and Self-Assurance — were very relationship-oriented, but he didn't think much of it.

So he buried himself in his schoolwork and focused on applying his strengths to his learning, which helped him get the most out of his classes. "Actually, the more attention I paid to my strengths and how I used them, the more I realized I'd kind of *always* used them at school, just not very well — kind of scattershot instead of deliberately," he says. "They work better if you aim them."

Still, during his first semester at school, Mauricio hadn't made any friends beyond his roommate, which worried his mother so much that she came for a lengthy visit. Mauricio admitted that he thought he would feel connected to the school just by living on campus. But having one friendship isn't the same thing as being fully engaged and connected to campus life. So, to make his mom feel better, he told her he would consider joining a group for engineering students on campus. "But meh," Mauricio says. "Their big thing was organizing a booth on career days, which is fine, but not what I'm into."

Weeks later, he noticed a student riding a skateboard on campus. Mauricio says, "He had a loaded Dervish Sama [skateboard] with Randall R-11 trucks, so I knew the dude wasn't playing." Mauricio followed the student on foot to a skate park a few blocks away. He called his mom and asked her to send him his longboard, and she did.

Mauricio started going to the park after class and riding his skateboard on campus — and he suddenly realized that his school had a big skater population. "It's like there was a hidden community of skaters here, people I can hang with, disguised as Midwesterners this whole time. I made more friends on a skateboard than I had in all of high school," he says.

Mauricio says he started feeling more confident and comfortable expanding his social circle to include non-skaters, even some ice fishermen. But the best part was that he felt like a welcome, contributing part of a community again. "My mom is so happy about it that she gave me a Dervish Sama as a Valentine's Day present," Mauricio says. "And she usually just sends cookies."

Mauricio is now a senior and wears his school's hoodies with pride. "The more involved I got here at school, the more comfortable I felt getting involved," he says. "So I joined the engineering group after all." It didn't take Mauricio long to figure out why the group was so lackluster and why its campus involvement was so minimal — Mauricio says that's his Analytical and Ideation at work. And his Self-Assurance gave him the confidence to get the club out of its rut. "This year, they elected me president. My mom is thrilled. And I got us to add a skateboarding clinic/engineering presentation at the career day. We had more people at our booth than the architecture students, and they were giving out pizza," he says.

Mauricio believes that he and his friends have created something that will continue to draw students in long after they graduate. And he loves giving back to the town and school. "Plus, we're creating the next generation of skaters and engineers," he says. "And that's important." When Mauricio got deeply involved on campus and used his strengths, it changed his entire college experience.

YOUR STRENGTHS AND LEADERSHIP

As you look beyond the experiences you have in college and start thinking about your career, get involved in leadership roles on campus. Employers look for leadership experience, and they will ask about it in job interviews. Maybe that means becoming the president of a club. Maybe you would prefer a behind-the-scenes role. Leadership isn't restricted to the position you have. You can lead from whatever role you have in a club or organization.

The good news is, you can apply any CliftonStrengths theme to leadership roles and responsibilities because they are all useful — even the themes that don't seem like it at first. For example, you can use Relator to understand team members' points of view so you can guide them better and include them more. You can use Input to collect all the information you need so you can make well-informed decisions. Context can show you where your group's purpose fits in the larger campus environment. So when you assume leadership roles in college, you can develop leadership strengths regardless of your top themes of talent.

Also, if you get the chance to manage others, take it. Managing people can be one of the most important aspects of leadership. Gallup has found that the most effective managers are those who capitalize on their greatest talents and consciously use them as they manage others.

If you look at great leaders such as Winston Churchill or Mahatma Gandhi, you will notice more differences than similarities — and the differences are what defined them. Churchill's bold and commanding leadership succeeded in mobilizing a war-ravaged nation. Gandhi's leadership during and after India's struggle for independence was based on peaceful resistance — the polar opposite of Churchill.

Both men knew their strengths and used them wisely. That's more unusual than you might think. All too often, leaders are blind to the obvious — their own personality. People who don't know their own strengths and weaknesses can develop self-concepts that are miles away from reality. Gallup has spoken with several leaders who claim to be great at developing their people, but their employees tell a very different story.

Although less noticeable than blind spots for weaknesses, blind spots for strengths are harmful too. Unfortunately, many leaders haven't discovered where they have the most potential for growth.

But you can. You've already started. And college gives you a magnificent opportunity to gain leadership experience that can lead to a more engaging career where you can use your strengths. The key is to be intentional. Look for every opportunity to refine your greatest talents in leadership roles.

Effective Teams and the Four Domains of Leadership Strength

Gallup has studied thousands of organizations and teams and found that the most cohesive and successful teams are the ones in which team members are aware of their own unique strengths as well as the strengths of each individual on the team.

Gallup also found that the 34 CliftonStrengths talent themes sort into four distinct domains of leadership strength: Executing, Influencing, Relationship Building and Strategic Thinking. While focusing on your top five themes is essential for your *individual* development, these broad domains or groupings of themes offer a practical way to look at the composition of a *team or group.*

Executing Themes	Achiever, Arranger, Belief, Consistency, Deliberative, Discipline, Focus, Responsibility, Restorative
Influencing Themes	Activator, Command, Communication, Competition, Maximizer, Self-Assurance, Significance, Woo
Relationship Building Themes	Adaptability, Connectedness, Developer, Empathy, Harmony, Includer, Individualization, Positivity, Relator
Strategic Thinking Themes	Analytical, Context, Futuristic, Ideation, Input, Intellection, Learner, Strategic

41

One way to examine a team's overall strength is to see how the individual members' top themes sort into the four domains. These categories can give you valuable insight into how team members contribute by describing how they make things happen, influence others, build relationships and work with information. Seeing their dominant talents grouped by domain helps everyone on the team understand how they think and act as individuals — as well as how the team's most dominant talents sort collectively.

It generally serves a group well to have a representation of strengths from multiple domains. Instead of one dominant leader who tries to do everything or a group of individuals who all have similar strengths, when team members' strengths come from multiple domains, the team is likely to be more effective and cohesive. Although individuals don't need to be well-rounded, partnerships and teams should be. A blend of strengths will help any group you belong to or lead get more done.

Think about your own top five themes. Where do they fall within the four domains of leadership strength? What kind of a leader are you? Do you have a lot of themes in one domain but none in another? How will you apply your unique talents to your leadership roles? How will you contribute to groups or teams where you are not the leader?

Now, think about the groups, teams and clubs you belong to on and off campus as well as all the leadership roles you play.

Looking at the four domains, how the 34 themes sort within them and the examples below, consider all the different ways everyone contributes to each group's overall success.

Executing: Leaders with dominant strength in this domain know how to make things happen. When you need someone to act, these are the people who will get things done.

For example, leaders with Deliberative or Discipline may excel at establishing a process and timetable for a group project, while different leaders will use their Achiever to work relentlessly toward a group's goal. Leaders with strong Arranger can determine the optimal way to use team members' strengths to complete a task.

Influencing: When you need someone to take charge, speak up and make sure your group is heard, look to leaders with the strength to influence. They can sell an idea, and they're excellent at communicating to different audiences: resident halls, sororities and fraternities, or athletic teams.

For example, campus leaders with a lot of Command or Self-Assurance might use few words, but their confidence will win followers. In contrast, leaders who use Communication or Woo can get people involved by making them feel comfortable and connected.

Relationship Building: Those who lead through Relationship Building are the essential glue that holds a team together.

Without these strengths on a team, the group is simply a bunch of individuals. Leaders with exceptional Relationship Building strengths have the ability to make a group much greater than the sum of its parts.

Leaders with Positivity can keep the team's collective energy high, and someone with Harmony will minimize disputes. Leaders with Individualization will see and respect each team member's specific interests. Leaders with strong Relator or Developer will push others toward bigger achievements.

Strategic Thinking: Leaders with Strategic Thinking strengths keep a team focused on what could be. They constantly absorb and analyze information, help the team make better decisions, and create a vision for the future.

Within this domain, leaders using Context or Strategic can explain how past events influenced present circumstances or navigate the best route for the future. They can help the team break old habits and create a new path toward change. Leaders with strong Ideation or Input might see countless opportunities for growth based on all of the information they review. And leaders drawing from their Analytical theme will help the team drill into the details and ask the perfect question at the perfect time.

STARTING THE JOURNEY

When you know your strengths, you know the value you bring to the world around you. You know when and where you're at your best. When you know your strengths, you have a holistic view of all the people and experiences that shape your life on campus and beyond.

SO NOW, IT'S UP TO YOU. IT'S YOUR STORY, YOUR JOURNEY AND YOUR FUTURE.

Part Two:

CliftonStrengths
Themes in Action

● ● ●

The following pages list all 34 CliftonStrengths themes of talent and action items for each theme. These action items will give you deeper insight into your top talent themes — and maybe even help you identify blind spots — so you can make the most of your college experience by using your strengths.

Achiever	Deliberative	Intellection
Activator	Developer	Learner
Adaptability	Discipline	Maximizer
Analytical	Empathy	Positivity
Arranger	Focus	Relator
Belief	Futuristic	Responsibility
Command	Harmony	Restorative
Communication	Ideation	Self-Assurance
Competition	Includer	Significance
Connectedness	Individualization	Strategic
Consistency	Input	Woo
Context		

Achiever

Your Achiever theme helps explain your drive. Achiever describes a constant need for achievement. You feel as if every day starts at zero. By the end of the day you must achieve something tangible in order to feel good about yourself. And by "every day" you mean every single day — workdays, weekends, vacations. No matter how much you may feel you deserve a day of rest, if the day passes without some form of achievement, no matter how small, you will feel dissatisfied. You have an internal fire burning inside you. It pushes you to do more, to achieve more. After each accomplishment is reached, the fire dwindles for a moment, but very soon it rekindles itself, forcing you toward the next accomplishment. Your relentless need for achievement might not be logical. It might not even be focused. But it will always be with you. As an Achiever you must learn to live with this whisper of discontent. It does have its benefits. It brings you the energy you need to work long hours without burning out. It is the jolt you can always count on to get you started on new tasks, new challenges. It is the power supply that causes you to set the pace and define the levels of productivity for your work group. It is the theme that keeps you moving.

Achiever Action Items

- Look for internships that will draw on your deep reservoir of internal motivation, stamina and determination.

- How often do you stop to celebrate your success before worrying about what's next? Remember to acknowledge your accomplishments — finishing a big project or acing an exam — before you move on to the next thing on your long to-do list.

- You are good at simplifying overwhelming projects into attainable steps, and that's a talent many groups need. Pay attention to bulletin boards around campus, and look for opportunities to join teams that need your ability to make complex tasks achievable.

- Join groups and clubs with members who have a strong work ethic. Working with others who share your drive for accomplishment will intensify your Achiever talents. You will challenge each other to excel and make the group stronger.

- Use your energy as efficiently as possible, and take regular study breaks so you can connect with others in person. Partner with someone with strong Discipline or Focus talents who can help you sort through your priorities.

- Intentionally form and nurture friendships with students in your classes or residence hall who are as driven as you are. These relationships will make you feel challenged and alive, and that will bring out the best in you.

- You likely have a to-do list for every day, week and month. Be careful not to take on too many goals at once. You need to be able to sustain your energy until you graduate, so try to pace yourself.

- What financial aid will you need this semester? How much debt do you have to carry to complete your degree? Create an itemized list to manage your debt accumulation and personal expenses. Every semester, review your financial to-do list to figure out if you are on track. Seeing the progress you make toward your financial goals over time will satisfy your Achiever talents.

- When you are working on a project or studying for long periods of time, be sure to take breaks. Get up and walk around to recharge. Your inner drive may cause you to lose track of time when you are working hard. If so, schedule breaks so you don't burn out.

- Even though you may feel like you don't need as much sleep as others, adequate sleep is essential to your health and is linked to learning retention and cognitive ability. You likely have a lot going on in your classes and on your own time. Make sure you get enough sleep so you will achieve everything on your list and more.

- At the next activity fair on campus, focus on clubs and organizations that have the kind of mission and values you are drawn to — those with ambitious goals or projects and measurable outcomes.

- Make the most of your determination by taking on a challenging volunteer opportunity. Explore organizations on and off campus that could benefit from your intense efforts and that link to your long-term career goals.

- Your Achiever talents will flourish in roles that challenge you and reward your hard work. Look for leadership opportunities on campus that offer career-related experience or that will add to your personal development — as well as bolster your résumé.

Activator

"When can we start?" This is a recurring question in your life. You are impatient for action. You may concede that analysis has its uses or that debate and discussion can occasionally yield some valuable insights, but deep down you know that only action is real. Only action can make things happen. Only action leads to performance. Once a decision is made, you cannot not act. Others may worry that "there are still some things we don't know," but this doesn't seem to slow you. If the decision has been made to go across town, you know that the fastest way to get there is to go stoplight to stoplight. You are not going to sit around waiting until all the lights have turned green. Besides, in your view, action and thinking are not opposites. In fact, guided by your Activator theme, you believe that action is the best device for learning. You make a decision, you take action, you look at the result and you learn. This learning informs your next action and your next. How can you grow if you have nothing to react to? Well, you believe you can't. You must put yourself out there. You must take the next step. It is the only way to keep your thinking fresh and informed. The bottom line is this: You know you will be judged not by what you say, not by what you think, but by what you get done. This does not frighten you. It pleases you.

Activator Action Items

- Your success hinges on being fully engaged. Choose courses that involve hands-on activities, lively verbal exchanges and interesting experiments. Your academic adviser will be able to help you identify dynamic courses.

- You have an ability to spark action and momentum in others. Be strategic with your Activator talents. Determine the best times, the best places and the best people with whom to use your valuable influence.

- Consider leading a study group for courses that you enjoy. Urge members to share their best ideas. Encourage quiet or timid people to explore topics, raise questions and contribute to projects.

- People with exceptional Activator talents like to jump right in and start, so your best approach to career planning is to try out various roles. Consider part-time jobs, work-study jobs or volunteer opportunities that let you "try on" a career that looks interesting to you.

- Look for something you can initiate this semester that will lead you closer to your career goals. A class, a job, a mentorship — find something that moves you forward.

- Encourage your friends and classmates to move their thoughts from concept to implementation. Whether they are considering taking a difficult class, looking for a new apartment or starting a relationship — or even if they have a great new idea — help them make a decision and start moving. Your push for action can inspire others to move forward, especially when they feel uncertain.

- Find a mentor with strong Focus, Futuristic, Strategic or Analytical talents. Complementary partnerships are valuable to everyone, but Activators don't always look before they leap. Partnering with people who can add direction and planning to your activation may help you build consensus, troubleshoot and get the outcomes you want.

- Make appointments with professors and teaching assistants to confirm expectations, clarify course requirements and establish deadlines. This kind of planning may feel like a speed bump in your rush to get started, but knowing what to expect before you activate can save you from a lot of trouble later.

- Consider becoming an entrepreneur. Make a list of possible businesses you could start, grow and sell once they show a profit. You may lose interest once an enterprise is so fine-tuned that it runs on its own. That's OK. Lots of people can run a business, but Activators have a special ability for getting them off the ground.

- Get enough sleep each night to make sure your memory and reasoning abilities are fully charged for the next day's classes. If you are not getting enough sleep, you may move to action too quickly without listening to others and thinking first.

- Volunteer for activities that require more than just meetings. Quick starters like you need to see results. See if you can get involved in building a Habitat for Humanity house, being a Big Brother or Big Sister, acting in community theater productions, leading nature walks, raising funds for worthwhile causes, or coaching a youth team.

- Be the change agent for a stalled project in the clubs or organizations you belong to. Study the original action plan, and determine why the team lost momentum. Convince group members that they can put the project back on course. You could even recruit energetic friends to help implement the new initiative.

- Run for office in campus government. You can probably think of a lot of things that would improve your school, and you have the drive to get the ball rolling. Recruit friends to help you campaign.

- Join clubs and try out for athletic teams with jam-packed rosters or events. Avoid groups that have a reputation for meeting a lot but not accomplishing much.

Adaptability

You live in the moment. You don't see the future as a fixed destination. Instead, you see it as a place that you create out of the choices that you make right now. And so you discover your future one choice at a time. This doesn't mean that you don't have plans. You probably do. But this theme of Adaptability does enable you to respond willingly to the demands of the moment even if they pull you away from your plans. Unlike some, you don't resent sudden requests or unforeseen detours. You expect them. They are inevitable. Indeed, on some level you actually look forward to them. You are, at heart, a very flexible person who can stay productive when the demands of work are pulling you in many different directions at once.

Adaptability Action Items

- Calm yourself before a stressful exam with positive self-talk. You've probably dealt with unwelcome surprises on tests before and done well. Recall your positive personal history, and embrace your ability to expect the unexpected to prep yourself for big tests, presentations or interviews.

- As you think about your major and your future career, avoid jobs or areas that demand a lot of structure and predictability. These roles may quickly frustrate you, make you feel inadequate and stifle your independence.

- Meet with a career counselor to look for an internship that requires flexibility. Many people need and rely on routine, but you are comfortable with rapid change. Capitalize on your ability to monitor and adjust. Your Adaptability talents could be a huge asset to many organizations.

- Surround yourself with individuals who, like you, pause to take in the world's beauty as it appears. Spending time with people who are willing to put aside what they are doing to watch a sunset or listen to the rain will invigorate your Adaptability talents.

- You are a co-traveler on the road of life. Your lack of a personal agenda helps others trust that you are truly there to participate with, rather than manipulate, them. Ask your roommates and friends questions about where they want to go in life, and help them get there. They will know that you are genuinely on their side.

- Look for a mentor to help you with planning. Someone with strong Focus or Strategic talents can help you shape your long-term career goals, leaving you to excel at dealing with your day-to-day intentions.

- You are comfortable with change, and you can provide stability for those who don't cope as well. Encourage your friends and family to talk to you when they have to modify or scrap their plans altogether. Listen closely and ask questions so you can help guide them through these changes.

- Avoid making impulse purchases. Ask yourself whether something is a "want" or a "need." If you can't tell which it is, take a walk around the block before you spend your money. A little time and perspective can help you make better choices.

- While you easily adjust to change, sometimes circumstances will require you to ride out a storm and keep your vision on long-term goals. When that happens, partner with friends or professors who have strong Futuristic, Maximizer or Discipline talents. They can keep you from making changes too quickly when you need to focus on the future.

- Explore fitness classes that are demanding but not stressful. You will be at your best in classes with people who have different fitness levels all seeking to improve in their own way. A yoga class may be just the thing for you. It's great for stress relief, there are a variety of different poses, you improve at your own pace and it focuses on living in the moment.

- Encourage a group of your friends to plan weekend outings together. Take turns picking the activity. You will love the variety of adventures, and you and your friends might get more exercise than you realize.

- Consider participating in extemporaneous speech tournaments or improvisational theater. Play to your ability to capitalize on each moment.

- Be thankful that you can balance your academic demands with your social commitments, extracurricular activities and job. Think about all the different requests on your time that you managed last week and the progress you made. Do you have any tips you could share with your friends?

- You live in the moment and don't mind modifications to existing plans as much as some people do. How can you help your peers who struggle with accepting change? Explain the benefits of letting go of an original plan to try a new one to help them understand the reasons for and advantages of the change.

Analytical

Your Analytical theme challenges other people: "Prove it. Show me why what you are claiming is true." In the face of this kind of questioning some will find that their brilliant theories wither and die. For you, this is precisely the point. You do not necessarily want to destroy other people's ideas, but you do insist that their theories be sound. You see yourself as objective and dispassionate. You like data because they are value free. They have no agenda. Armed with these data, you search for patterns and connections. You want to understand how certain patterns affect one another. How do they combine? What is their outcome? Does this outcome fit with the theory being offered or the situation being confronted? These are your questions. You peel the layers back until, gradually, the root cause or causes are revealed. Others see you as logical and rigorous. Over time they will come to you in order to expose someone's "wishful thinking" or "clumsy thinking" to your refining mind. It is hoped that your analysis is never delivered too harshly. Otherwise, others may avoid you when that "wishful thinking" is their own.

Analytical Action Items

- What is the difference between when you are academically successful and when you're not? Evaluate your study habits, note taking, listening, capacity for asking questions and reading comprehension. Your analysis will sharpen your studying techniques so you can improve your odds for future success.

- Analyze and record your thoughts as you read and study. Ask: What is missing here? What questions should the author have answered? What biases are evident and not so evident? Using your natural tendency to scrutinize and investigate will help you comprehend what you are studying.

- Data and evidence are a source of security for you. If the research backs it, then you are willing to accept a plan and its consequences. Carefully examine your options in all areas of your life. Your deep analysis of what is possible — or not — will make you more confident about your future.

- You tend to break things down into their component parts. Stretch your Analytical talents by thinking about how someone older than you would interpret the same set of facts — or someone younger than you or from a different cultural, ethnic, religious, socio-economic or racial background.

- Interview people who are in careers that interest you. One hallmark of Analytical talents is the quality of your questions. Put your talent to ask smart questions to good use when selecting a career.

- You automatically uncover what's real, true and honest. Your friends and family will count on you to be the "truth finder" when information or circumstances conflict or confuse. Think of your Analytical talents as one way you can support others, and don't wait for them to ask for help.

- Your mind is constantly working and producing insightful analysis. Are your friends and classmates aware of that? Find the best way to express your thoughts: writing, one-on-one conversations or group discussions. Put value to your thoughts by communicating them.

- Your natural skepticism and need to see the evidence can lead you into lively debates that are part of your process for becoming convinced. However, not everyone enjoys debating issues as much as you do. Team up with friends or classmates who are exceptionally talented in Relator, Empathy or Communication, for instance, so that others understand you are critiquing ideas and not the people who have the ideas.

- Identify your biases before taking sides on an issue. Evaluate your own thinking before you challenge others.

- Guidance can be mutual. Collaborate with people who have strong Activator talents. You can help them make wise, considered decisions. They can help you turn your analysis into action.

- Make sense of the complexities of life by objectively talking through the pros and cons of the decisions you make. When you bring reason and objectivity to emotional situations, you can find solutions and reduce stress.

- Create a workout plan for yourself. Research different exercises, and take note of what muscles you are using for each one. Recording the connections between effort and results will help you come up with the most logical way to go about your routine. Then ask a personal trainer for feedback about your ideas and how you can improve them.

- Consider joining the debate team or taking classes that include pro and con discussions about issues that matter to you. To prepare for each debate and clarify your position, examine data, collect facts and read about the issue. Try to anticipate problems. Fully research both sides of the issue, and prepare logical arguments from both perspectives.

- When friends tell you about their problems, you may have the immediate urge to try to solve them. But sometimes your friends may just want you to listen. Respect their need to share without analysis. Remember that if they want your help coming up with solutions, they will ask for it.

Arranger

You are a conductor. When faced with a complex situation involving many factors, you enjoy managing all of the variables, aligning and realigning them until you are sure you have arranged them in the most productive configuration possible. In your mind there is nothing special about what you are doing. You are simply trying to figure out the best way to get things done. But others, lacking this theme, will be in awe of your ability. "How can you keep so many things in your head at once?" they will ask. "How can you stay so flexible, so willing to shelve well-laid plans in favor of some brand-new configuration that has just occurred to you?" But you cannot imagine behaving in any other way. You are a shining example of effective flexibility, whether you are changing travel schedules at the last minute because a better fare has popped up or mulling over just the right combination of people and resources to accomplish a new project. From the mundane to the complex, you are always looking for the perfect configuration. Of course, you are at your best in dynamic situations. Confronted with the unexpected, some complain that plans devised with such care cannot be changed, while others take refuge in the existing rules or procedures. You don't do either. Instead, you jump into the confusion, devising new options, hunting for new paths of least resistance and figuring out new partnerships — because, after all, there might just be a better way.

Arranger Action Items

- Prioritize your studies. Identify the most important tasks based on deadlines, percentage of final grade and difficulty. You will likely be able to concentrate better and study more effectively when you have arranged your classwork in the most productive way.

- Your mental juggling is instinctive, but some people might find it difficult to break with the status quo. Give your professors, friends and classmates time to understand your way of doing things when you present it to them.

- There is an inherent flexibility in your Arranger talents, so your ability to deal with many things at once might be most advantageous in stressful or chaotic situations. Visit the career center to look for internships that require multitasking and that can be relatively unpredictable.

- Organize routine activities, trips and parties for your residence hall, fraternity or sorority. Consider off-campus venues that let you take advantage of the discounts that come with your student ID. You will enjoy arranging details and schedules, and you and your friends will save money while having fun. Partner with someone with strong Ideation talents to make the events even more fun and creative.

- Do you schedule study breaks to clear your mind? Consider blocking off time to make phone calls, to meet with your friends, to go for a walk or to hit a workout class.

- Visit with your academic adviser to find a mentor who is interactive as well as collaborative. A dynamic relationship will help your talents flourish and grow.

- Read all of your degree requirements before enrolling in classes each semester. Are you on the most financially efficient path to completing your degree? Meet with your adviser to ask questions and make sure that your plan is the most cost-effective way to get your degree.

- Even the best exercise routines can be more efficient. If you already have a workout routine, use your Arranger talents to find new exercises that will not only challenge you but give you more streamlined results. If you don't have a workout plan, talk with the campus trainer about creating a routine that would be most effective for you.

- Being a student involves juggling multiple realities, which is likely easier for you than for others. Make the most of your natural flexibility and talent to cope with unpredictable circumstances to alleviate mental stress. Offer to help your classmates and friends as well.

- What activities, clubs or organizations are you involved in? Managing constant change is exhausting for a lot of people, but you get a kick out of it. Think about how you can use this valuable asset to help the groups you are in become more efficient and effective. Make a list of all the variables you need to manage, and volunteer to be the coordinator for the group.

- Get involved on campus or in your community, and stay busy. Explore community service opportunities where you could help arrange routine activities, special events or projects.

- Mix and match the talents, knowledge, skill and experience of your classmates to launch a new group project. Use your natural talent to arrange people and align priorities to create maximum efficiency, and be sure to explain your reasoning so others don't think you are trying to be controlling.

- You will thrive when your Arranger talents are energized, and you will suffer when they are bored. Look for résumé-building opportunities that will motivate you and allow your talent to manage complex situations to flourish.

Belief

If you possess a strong Belief theme, you have certain core values that are enduring. These values vary from one person to another, but ordinarily your Belief theme causes you to be family-oriented, altruistic, even spiritual, and to value responsibility and high ethics — both in yourself and others. These core values affect your behavior in many ways. They give your life meaning and satisfaction; in your view, success is more than money and prestige. They provide you with direction, guiding you through the temptations and distractions of life toward a consistent set of priorities. This consistency is the foundation for all your relationships. Your friends call you dependable. "I know where you stand," they say. Your Belief makes you easy to trust. It also demands that you find work that meshes with your values. Your work must be meaningful; it must matter to you. And guided by your Belief theme it will matter only if it gives you a chance to live out your values.

Belief Action Items

- Write an academic mission statement for yourself that integrates your core values — for example, leaving the world better than you found it, curing cancer, ending violence or affirming the dignity of each human being.

- Form a study group of other students with whom you share one or more important belief. Ask your study partners to describe how their fundamental principles contribute to their success in school.

- How can you weave your core values into routine classroom assignments? Try to research, write and speak about topics directly related to your beliefs.

- Choose courses taught by professors who are known for their strong beliefs, even when their values clash with yours. Learning about the beliefs of others can help you refine your own. Take the time to listen to those who see the world differently than you do.

- Think about your "calling." Once you have articulated your mission, seek more information at the career center on work that can help you fulfill it. Or look for clubs on campus that align with your purpose and objectives.

- Ask your friends and roommates to tell you when your passion inspires them and when it overwhelms them. Sometimes you might reveal your values through your actions and without words. Maintain an ongoing dialogue to ensure that you are understood *and* understanding. People who meet you for the first time may not understand where your intensity is coming from.

- Make sure that you are balancing your educational demands and your personal life. Your devotion to your studies should not come at the expense of your strong commitment to your family and friends — and vice versa.

- Don't be afraid to give voice to your beliefs in class or in social situations. Sharing your outlook on life will help others know who you are, where you stand and how to relate to you. New friends and classmates will also come to learn that they can depend on you.

- Find a mentor, or become a mentor. A mentoring relationship can give you valuable insight into the fit between who you are and what you were meant to do with your life. These insights can increase the chances for your behaviors, decisions and beliefs to remain congruent throughout your life.

- Collaborate with friends or classmates who have strong Futuristic talents. These partners can energize you by painting a vivid picture of the direction in which your values will lead.

- Debate an issue like "Money is the true source of happiness." Explore your Belief talents by arguing for and against this proposition. Ask yourself, "How did I strengthen my position when I incorporated my beliefs into the argument? How did I weaken my position when I had to defend the opposing point of view?" Think about how it feels to see things from another perspective.

- Consider running for student government. Build your campaign platform on values-oriented issues that matter greatly to you. A friend with strong Analytical or Communication talents can help you craft campaign materials and speeches to inform potential voters of what you stand for and why.

- Environments that are a good fit with your mission and beliefs will bring out your best. Look for opportunities to volunteer or intern with companies and organizations that exhibit a strong sense of mission. In particular, think about organizations that define their purpose by the contribution they make to society.

Command

Command leads you to take charge. Unlike some people, you feel no discomfort with imposing your views on others. On the contrary, once your opinion is formed, you need to share it with others. Once your goal is set, you feel restless until you have aligned others with you. You are not frightened by confrontation; rather, you know that confrontation is the first step toward resolution. Whereas others may avoid facing up to life's unpleasantness, you feel compelled to present the facts or the truth, no matter how unpleasant it may be. You need things to be clear between people and challenge them to be clear-eyed and honest. You push them to take risks. You may even intimidate them. And while some may resent this, labeling you opinionated, they often willingly hand you the reins. People are drawn toward those who take a stance and ask them to move in a certain direction. Therefore, people will be drawn to you. You have presence. You have Command.

Command Action Items

- What probing and pointed questions can you ask in class discussions and lectures? Realize that your questioning mind accelerates your learning, and when you ask a question rather than make a statement, others can learn as well.

- Take charge of your college education. Play the lead role in shaping your degree or certification plan. Make sure to confirm your strategy with your adviser, professors and mentors.

- When choosing your major, think about how you can use your Command talents to make a difference in the lives of others. Research the fields and organizations that would benefit most from your candid words and strong values. Consider your impact on the future.

- You don't need to confront all obstacles that come your way; there are some you can circumvent. Find a mentor with strong Woo, Strategic or Empathy talents. This person can help you identify and bypass unnecessary hurdles that can slow you down.

- Sometimes others see the tough exterior of your Command talents and assume it's an impenetrable shell. But healthy relationships depend on mutual trust and openness. Share your pain and struggles with friends and family. Letting others see vulnerabilities that your Command talents may disguise gives them equal power in the relationship and shows that you're trustworthy.

- How do your classmates and roommates react when your Command talents are in full force? Ask them for feedback about how others perceive you. Use your powerful demeanor to clarify rather than intimidate. While your words flow naturally and confidently, sometimes your Command talents are most effective when you ask questions and allow others time to think.

- Study your mannerisms, vocal tone and content of your messages when you talk with authority figures. Identify how you present yourself as someone who deserves their time and attention. How do you show them that you're a person of integrity whom they can trust? Ask them for feedback about what you see in yourself.

- Because you are comfortable bringing to light what others often avoid or don't say, you are good at resolving conflicts and misunderstandings. You have likely helped settle disputes between your friends or roommates. Appreciate the power of your ability to "clear the air" for others.

- Always go to class — not only because you're paying for it, but because you want to be heard. Use your Command talents to initiate great discussions and interactions. You can help everyone in class learn more by bringing out others' voices.

- You probably take pride in your ability to use the right words at the right time. But when you are stressed and your mind is racing, words don't always come out the right way. When you feel overwhelmed by school or other obligations, try exercising. A daily workout can clear your mind, reduce stress and help you articulate your thoughts.

- Is there a group on campus that needs help raising money for school projects? Use your Command talents to figure out how to get others to contribute to the group's cause.

- Participate in activities and classes that require you to persuade people to embrace your ideas, plans, solutions or philosophies. Talents become strengths when they have a foundation of skills and knowledge, and "selling" an idea is a great way to get the skills and knowledge you need to turn your Command talents into a strength.

- Consider running for a leadership position, like a representative for your student government, multicultural organization or residence hall council. Partner with people who have exceptional talents in themes such as Ideation and Strategic. They can help you see the big picture and become even more persuasive.

- Start a student group on campus that aligns with your personal mission. Use your powerful, inspirational words to get others to join. Talk about why the group's mission is important. Your emotion can motivate others to rise to the occasion and contribute their own time and talents. They may be counting on you to give voice to the passions that surround the cause.

- Explore your career options by trying out various volunteer roles. Your Command talents are likely to flourish in jobs that regularly deal with crises or rapid decision-making.

Communication

You like to explain, to describe, to host, to speak in public and to write. This is your Communication theme at work. Ideas are a dry beginning. Events are static. You feel a need to bring them to life, to energize them, to make them exciting and vivid. And so you turn events into stories and practice telling them. You take the dry idea and enliven it with images and examples and metaphors. You believe that most people have a very short attention span. They are bombarded by information, but very little of it survives. You want your information — whether an idea, an event, a product's features and benefits, a discovery, or a lesson — to survive. You want to divert their attention toward you and then capture it, lock it in. This is what drives your hunt for the perfect phrase. This is what draws you toward dramatic words and powerful word combinations. This is why people like to listen to you. Your word pictures pique their interest, sharpen their world and inspire them to act.

Communication Action Items

- How do you capture your audience's interest? Try telling stories that clarify an idea, theory, scientific law, philosophical point or ethical quandary. Entertain your study group with anecdotes that make math, history, science, languages or the arts come alive in their minds. Your lively stories will help them learn and retain what they study.

- When you're presenting in class, pay close attention to your classmates and professor. Watch their reactions to each part of your presentation. You will notice that some areas are especially engaging. Afterward, identify the moments that really caught the audience's attention. Draft your next presentation around these highlights.

- Which of your professors are good listeners? Meet with them several times throughout the term, and take advantage of the fact that they expect you to do most of the talking. You crave the undivided attention good listeners provide, and these conversations will energize your Communication talents.

- When you were engaged in conversation today, did you notice how people reacted to what you said? Did you capture their attention or get them to laugh? Use your Communication talents to draw others in, especially those who are new to a group.

- What are your friends' and roommates' values, philosophical views, goals, pet peeves and opinions? Learn more about each other to deepen your relationships. Use your gift for words to ask the perfect questions to get them talking about themselves.

- Some people think before they speak, and others think while they speak. You're probably among the latter — you think out loud to process your ideas with others. Look for friends, professors or classmates to be the audience you need to talk things through.

- Find a friend or mentor with a lot of Empathy talent. This person can remind you to consider others' feelings when you are talking with them, which will make you a more thoughtful and effective conversationalist. Practice active listening to show others that their opinions matter to you.

- You have the talent to find words for people's emotions — sometimes words they cannot find themselves. Pinpoint the key issues your friends or classmates are trying to communicate and the joys or struggles they want to convey. Then give voice to those feelings. Helping others find the words to express and process their own emotions is a powerful way to support them.

- If you enjoy writing, consider joining the school newspaper staff. If you enjoy public speaking, enroll in classes that require presentations. You delight in sharing your thoughts with others, so find the medium that best fits your voice and message. Your Communication talents will help you find just the right way to frame your ideas and state your case.

- Audition for plays even if you are not a theater major. Acting will teach you new ways to use your words, nonverbal communication and movement. All these novel ways to communicate will refine your thoughts and help you tell your stories.

- Consider becoming the spokesperson for an organization, club, nonprofit or product. Using your Communication talents to publicly represent something you believe in might open doors for future careers.

- Find leaders or professors on campus whom you admire for their ability to draw people in with their words. Ask them for a leadership role in their class or group. Pay attention to their communication style — the words they choose, their timing and their expressions. Not only will leadership experience look good on your résumé, but you will enjoy learning from these leaders' powerful messages.

- Volunteer at local organizations with missions that align with your values and that allow for significant social interaction. You are at your best when you can process your thoughts verbally with others. You may also learn better with others than you do alone.

Competition

Competition is rooted in comparison. When you look at the world, you are instinctively aware of other people's performance. Their performance is the ultimate yardstick. No matter how hard you tried, no matter how worthy your intentions, if you reached your goal but did not outperform your peers, the achievement feels hollow. Like all competitors, you need other people. You need to compare. If you can compare, you can compete, and if you can compete, you can win. And when you win, there is no feeling quite like it. You like measurement because it facilitates comparisons. You like other competitors because they invigorate you. You like contests because they must produce a winner. You particularly like contests where you know you have the inside track to be the winner. Although you are gracious to your fellow competitors and even stoic in defeat, you don't compete for the fun of competing. You compete to win. Over time you will come to avoid contests where winning seems unlikely.

Competition Action Items

- Identify a high-achieving person or people against whom you can measure your own achievement — a classmate, teammate or someone you admire. You need measurement to know if you are winning. And finding others to compare yourself with is the first step.

- What are your most meaningful academic goals? Design a system to keep track of your progress on reaching them. Measuring your achievement will motivate you to reach the highest levels of productivity, mastery and quality.

- Clarify how professors weight class participation, final exams, presentations, laboratory experiments and research projects. Continuously monitor your grades and class standing. You will be more engaged in your classes when you know the score.

- Do you prefer to compete as an individual or as a team member? Do you want to share control of final results, or do you want to be the only one in control? Select an internship that matches your preferences.

- Explore different professions at the campus career center. Then compare yourself to people who are successful in the fields that interest you. What do they have that you don't — education, skills, experience?

Figure out what you need to be just as successful as they are so when you choose your career, you will already have a plan to win.

- Help your roommates and classmates understand that you are hardwired to have the last word in casual conversations, classroom discussions or formal debates. Ask them to kindly remind you when it's time to pause, listen and respect what others are saying.

- Engage fellow competitors in your residence hall in a fun weekly competition. By taking on a challenge together, you can create lasting connections based on mutual interests and a shared reprieve from the pressures of college.

- Build a partnership with someone on campus who has strong Strategic talents. Strategic partners can increase your odds for success by helping you think through options and obstacles that could get in your way — and help you plot a path to victory.

- Invite someone you like to compete against to go with you to a fitness class or on a hike. Set goals, and compete with each other to see who can reach them first. You will enjoy the friendly rivalry and get a workout as well.

- Design some mental strategies that can help you deal with a loss. Armed with these strategies, you will be able to move on to the next challenge more quickly. Consider meditation, yoga, journaling and mindfulness.

- Play competitive sports. Risk being a walk-on player to earn a spot on an athletic team. Find a university club or intramural team if you want to compete at a different level. Participating in sports has many benefits: It's a great way to get exercise, you'll meet new people and you get a chance to compete — and win.

- Run for leadership positions such as a seat on the student senate, class president, club officer or sorority/fraternity chair. Campaign to win.

- A winning or successful team creates contagious confidence. How can you help people in the clubs or organizations you belong to be their best? Align team members so that they're building on their strengths; this gives them the best possible chance for success and confidence. And when they win, you win.

- Remember that not everyone assigns the same emotional intensity to every activity like you do. Make sure to demonstrate that you accept and respect other people's reasons for being involved.

Connectedness

Things happen for a reason. You are sure of it. You are sure of it because in your soul you know that we are all connected. Yes, we are individuals, responsible for our own judgments and in possession of our own free will, but nonetheless we are part of something larger. Some may call it the collective unconscious. Others may label it spirit or life force. But whatever your word of choice, you gain confidence from knowing that we are not isolated from one another or from the earth and the life on it. This feeling of Connectedness implies certain responsibilities. If we are all part of a larger picture, then we must not harm others because we will be harming ourselves. We must not exploit because we will be exploiting ourselves. Your awareness of these responsibilities creates your value system. You are considerate, caring and accepting. Certain of the unity of humankind, you are a bridge builder for people of different cultures. Sensitive to the invisible hand, you can give others comfort that there is a purpose beyond our humdrum lives. The exact articles of your faith will depend on your upbringing and your culture, but your faith is strong. It sustains you and your close friends in the face of life's mysteries.

Connectedness Action Items

- Look for links between your coursework and your contribution to the human family now and in the future. Ask yourself what life lessons you are supposed to learn through your studies and the challenges they present. What is as — or more — important as passing a test or getting a good grade?

- What is your mission in life? Share this calling with your friends, and ask them what their purpose is. These stimulating and inspiring conversations might help other people see connections in their own lives and can renew your own sense of purpose.

- Use service-learning opportunities to explore possible careers that interest you. For example, spend your summers volunteering for humanitarian causes to determine the best fit for your talents.

- Talk with your mentor about the connections you see between your classes, your major, your values and your mission. A mentor — whether an instructor, coach or career adviser — can be a valuable sounding board as you articulate the synergy that you see so naturally.

- Explain to your roommates and friends how and why you can remain calm in the midst of uncertainty. How do they react to ambiguity — in classwork, relationships or dealing with professors? When life isn't black and white, use your confidence that everything will work out to help those who are struggling.

- Don't spend too much time trying to persuade others to have the same holistic worldview that you do. You see the world as a linked web. Your sense of connection is intuitive. If others don't share your intuition, you will most likely not convince them to.

- It may surprise you when others don't see the connections you do. Try to explain the interrelatedness you are so sure of to your friends and classmates. Challenge them to think in new ways and broaden their worldview. Ask them to think about how they could take their talent to a new level by applying it somewhere new or how they might partner with someone they see as much different from themselves.

- Look for friends with strong Communication talents. They can help you find the words you need to describe vivid examples of connection in the real world. What you may feel, they can describe.

- Help your friends and classmates see the connections between their talents, their actions, their mission and the success of a larger group. When people believe in what they're doing and feel like part of something bigger, they will be more committed to the overall cause.

- You are aware of the boundaries and borders that organizational structure can impose, but you treat them as seamless and fluid. Use your Connectedness talents to break down walls that prevent knowledge sharing across clubs, groups and organizations on campus. Encourage different groups to work together for their shared goals.

- Consider developing the mission statement for an organization or club. You naturally feel like you are part of something larger than yourself, and contributing to an overall statement or goal might be very rewarding for you.

- Values can be a strong foundation when you share them with others. If values are integral to your relationship with another person or group, your natural confidence and assurance may be crucial in times of uncertainty or fear. Be ready to reach out when you notice that others need your support.

- Join clubs or volunteer at organizations that will allow you to incorporate your need to serve people. Religious, environmental, political, social — whatever the purpose, being involved with groups that share your values will give you the deep sense of meaning that is so important to you.

Consistency

Balance is important to you. You are keenly aware of the need to treat people the same, no matter what their station in life, so you do not want to see the scales tipped too far in any one person's favor. In your view this leads to selfishness and individualism. It leads to a world where some people gain an unfair advantage because of their connections or their background or their greasing of the wheels. This is truly offensive to you. You see yourself as a guardian against it. In direct contrast to this world of special favors, you believe that people function best in a consistent environment where the rules are clear and are applied to everyone equally. This is an environment where people know what is expected. It is predictable and evenhanded. It is fair. Here each person has an even chance to show their worth.

Consistency Action Items

- What do you need to do to earn the grade you want in each class? Set up and adhere to a study routine. You excel when your life has a rhythm to it.

- When considering different internships, try to find companies that have clearly established regulations, policies, procedures and guidelines. You are likely to feel more comfortable, effective and efficient in structured environments than you would in less controlled settings.

- Talk to your friends and roommates about your need for uniformity, but don't make it all about you. Verbalize why fairness and following rules are so important to you — then listen. People have their own needs, and it's only fair to compromise if you have different opinions.

- Being able to predict how another person will act — and react — helps you confidently plot the course for a relationship. Think about how your Consistency talents influence your relationships with others. Are you always there in times of need? Do you consistently show compassion and caring?

- Make friends with someone in your residence hall who has powerful Individualization talents. This person can remind you when it's appropriate and important to accommodate individual differences.

- Cultivate a reputation around campus for acknowledging people who deserve credit. Become the conscience of your classes or of the organizations or groups you belong to. You will naturally make sure that any praise is genuine — and that those who truly contributed get the recognition.

- Use your Consistency talents now to develop rules, policies and procedures that will remain with you throughout your life.

- You are naturally aware of when things are out of balance, and you can quickly restore stability. Once you figure out the best way to find balance, keep doing it — especially when you are in a stressful situation.

- Referee intramural athletic events, or help create policies in your residence hall. Applying the same rules to everyone brings out your best.

- In the clubs or organizations you belong to, keep your focus on others' performance. Your Consistency talents might occasionally lead you to overemphasize *how* others get work done and ignore *what* they get done.

- You are a watchdog for social justice. Consider joining groups on campus or in your community that focus on equality and human rights issues. You might have the unique ability to push your cause forward while at the same time practicing restraint. Help guide your group patiently, and be careful about forcing change too quickly.

- Structured, predictable, detail-oriented environments are likely to appeal to you. Look for volunteer opportunities in organizations that value loyalty and that apply policies equally to everyone. You will be more productive in settings that emphasize consistency.

- A level playing field is the only kind you want. Join campus or community groups that provide disadvantaged people with the platform they need to show their true potential.

Context

You look back. You look back because that is where the answers lie. You look back to understand the present. From your vantage point the present is unstable, a confusing clamor of competing voices. It is only by casting your mind back to an earlier time, a time when the plans were being drawn up, that the present regains its stability. The earlier time was a simpler time. It was a time of blueprints. As you look back, you begin to see these blueprints emerge. You realize what the initial intentions were. These blueprints or intentions have since become so embellished that they are almost unrecognizable, but now this Context theme reveals them again. This understanding brings you confidence. No longer disoriented, you make better decisions because you sense the underlying structure. You become a better partner because you understand how your colleagues came to be who they are. And counterintuitively you become wiser about the future because you saw its seeds being sown in the past. Faced with new people and new situations, it will take you a little time to orient yourself, but you must give yourself this time. You must discipline yourself to ask the questions and allow the blueprints to emerge because no matter what the situation, if you haven't seen the blueprints, you will have less confidence in your decisions.

Context Action Items

- Before writing papers or starting class projects, ask your professors for examples of excellent work so you can see how others successfully approached the assignment.

- Register for courses such as comparative religion, geography, economics, science or philosophy to better understand the root causes of today's wars, alliances, financial policies, treaties and trade agreements.

- How would you describe your history of test taking? Look for patterns, and identify your best performances. Prepare for today's exams by replicating study techniques that worked for you in the past.

- History is an obvious field of study for people with strong Context talents. But you can fulfill your career needs in many other fields that would benefit from your way of thinking — law, city planning, social work, theater arts and education. Ask your mentor or academic adviser to help you explore your career options in depth and give you feedback.

- The roots, history and formative moments in people's lives intrigue you. Ask new friends or classmates questions to elicit stories that will be as fun for you to hear as they are for others to tell. Showing an interest in their life demonstrates that you care and will make your relationship stronger.

- When other students are struggling with a difficult choice or challenge, ask them about how they dealt with a similar situation in the past. Your insightful questions can help them get perspective and guide them away from making recurring mistakes. Helping others recognize the strength they have demonstrated in the past can give them hope and confidence now and in the future.

- Because you value lessons of the past so much, you may have a tendency to feel that you need to do things the way they have always been done. If you have a hard time with change, find a mentor with powerful Maximizer talents who can help you improve on your existing methods and habits.

- Talk to people you admire in fields that interest you about the decisions and changes they made that led them to their career, whether you know them or not. You'd be surprised at how many people — even busy and successful people — will make time to offer their guidance.

- Partner with students who have exceptional Futuristic talents. They can help you build an even stronger bridge from the past to the future.

- Learn about the personal and academic experiences of the people on your teams and in your study groups.

Knowing their background will make you more comfortable working with them.

- Think about your past successes and the effective coping mechanisms you have used. What did you learn from them that you could apply today? Consider volunteering your talents to peer counseling services on your campus that can help with a variety of issues, for example, academic stress, relationship problems and anxiety.

- Serve as the historian for your fraternity, sorority, honor society or other campus group. Help strengthen your club's culture by understanding its roots. For example, collect symbols and stories that represent the best of the past. You know that the values and goals of your group are based on the wisdom of its alumni and their traditions. Share your insights of the past with other group members to guide and inspire them in the present.

- Form a book club with friends and classmates who also have strong Context talents. Read and then discuss autobiographies, biographies, history books or historical fiction. You will enjoy studying the origins and accounts of others' lives and past events. Understanding the roots helps you understand the results.

Deliberative

You are careful. You are vigilant. You are a private person. You know that the world is an unpredictable place. Everything may seem in order, but beneath the surface you sense the many risks. Rather than denying these risks, you draw each one out into the open. Then each risk can be identified, assessed and ultimately reduced. Thus, you are a fairly serious person who approaches life with a certain reserve. For example, you like to plan ahead so as to anticipate what might go wrong. You select your friends cautiously and keep your own counsel when the conversation turns to personal matters. You are careful not to give too much praise and recognition, lest it be misconstrued. If some people don't like you because you are not as effusive as others, then so be it. For you, life is not a popularity contest. Life is something of a minefield. Others can run through it recklessly if they so choose, but you take a different approach. You identify the dangers, weigh their relative impact and then place your feet deliberately. You walk with care.

Deliberative Action Items

- Do you know what your professors, coaches or friends expect from you today? Plan ahead to minimize unknown factors. Contact your professors or classmates if you are unsure about expectations for your classes or projects. You will be better prepared when you have time to prioritize your actions and think about the possible outcomes of those actions.

- You are most comfortable in structured settings. Look for professors and classes that offer clear expectations, consistent weekly discussions and the freedom for you to think about how to contribute ahead of time.

- Before visiting with a professor, prepare thoroughly by making a list of all the things you want to discuss and all the questions you want to ask. You will feel more confident if you are prepared.

- You probably are good at examining others' actions and helping them think through their decisions before they move ahead too quickly. Look for internships or mentoring opportunities that would let you use those talents every day.

- Find friends or classmates with strong Command, Self-Assurance or Activator talents. While you carefully weigh the risks and rewards of each step you take, these partners can help you face tough choices more quickly and with confidence. The decisions you make together will be sound.

- During times of change or confusion, remember the advantages of your conservative decision-making process. Instead of making reactionary choices, you think through all of the pros and cons, minimizing risk. Apply your caution and care to help your friends when they are struggling with a decision or when they feel like their lives are chaotic.

- You might not enjoy purely social activities. Still, you might feel left out when everybody but you is going to a party, even if you don't want to go. Everyone needs to be part of a community, and there are a lot of different ways to socialize. Find an activity that's fun but also meaningful to you. See if your favorite classmates want to start a discussion group. Or have lunch with friends from your residence hall to talk about upcoming events or weekend plans.

- How much debt will you accumulate during college? You are a rigorous thinker. Identify any land mines that could derail your plans to graduate with a manageable student loan debt.

- Keep track of all your academic deadlines. For you, unknown deadlines may lead to unhealthy stress. When you receive a class syllabus, highlight the due dates of readings, assignments, papers and exams.

- You inspire trust because you are cautious and considerate about sensitive topics. Look for leadership roles in organizations that deal with delicate issues and conflicts. Any group that handles money from dues or fundraisers would benefit from your assistance. The campus health center might be a good place for a work-study job.

- You can be selective in your relationships. And it's probably very important to you that others' values align with yours. Look for somewhere to volunteer that has a stable core team of people and a culture and principles that you agree with.

- Check with people in your residence hall to find campus organizations or clubs you could join. Do you have any friends who have belonged to an organization for a long time you could talk to? Before you commit to joining, attend a couple of meetings to narrow down your options to one or two that seem to fit you best. Then give yourself a deadline to make your final decision.

- What résumé-building experiences are you looking for in clubs, classes and volunteer opportunities? Consider decision-making or risk-assessment roles to highlight what you do best.

Developer

You see the potential in others. Very often, in fact, potential is all you see. In your view no individual is fully formed. On the contrary, each individual is a work in progress, alive with possibilities. And you are drawn toward people for this very reason. When you interact with others, your goal is to help them experience success. You look for ways to challenge them. You devise interesting experiences that can stretch them and help them grow. And all the while you are on the lookout for the signs of growth — a new behavior learned or modified, a slight improvement in a skill, a glimpse of excellence or of "flow" where previously there were only halting steps. For you these small increments — invisible to some — are clear signs of potential being realized. These signs of growth in others are your fuel. They bring you strength and satisfaction. Over time many will seek you out for help and encouragement because on some level they know that your helpfulness is both genuine and fulfilling to you.

Developer Action Items

- Choose classes with a field-studies component that involves working with people. This will give you an opportunity to see others' tangible growth experiences outside the classroom.

- Reflect on what you have learned from your favorite professors and how they have influenced your life. Take the time to write and tell them about the specific impact their classes and teaching style have had on your personal development.

- One of the best ways to reinforce your own learning is to teach others. Try studying by yourself first so you can get a solid grasp on your coursework and assignments. Then offer to tutor classmates who are struggling. You will enjoy helping them learn and grow, and you will increase your chances for better grades as well.

- What is your personal mission? How can you connect your mission with your Developer talents to make a meaningful difference in other people's lives? Explore careers where you can help others reach their potential.

- Sometimes people with strong Developer talents apply them to others so much that they forget they are growing too. Remember to develop yourself. You cannot give what you do not have — it's OK to put your needs first. Who has helped you grow? Find a mentor or professor who will focus on your development.

- Consider becoming a counselor in your residence hall. This is a great opportunity and environment for you to talk with other students and help them grow academically and socially.

- Coach friends who have a specific goal or focus in mind, such as running a marathon or losing weight. Encourage them in their progress.

- Challenge your roommates and friends by asking them questions that stretch their imagination. What are their dreams? How much could they do if there were no barriers to their choices? You have likely already seen glimpses of their potential. Help them see it too.

- You might find that you are counseling more people than you can handle. To balance your inner drive with your academic priorities, consider the power of being a "mentor for the moment." Sometimes, just saying the right words at the right time can be a meaningful developmental moment for someone. Don't be afraid to offer spontaneous advice and encouragement; you might change someone's life.

- Seek out a mentor with strong Individualization talents. This person can show you where your greatest talents lie and help you focus your academic or career path. Without this perspective, your Developer instincts might lead you to concentrate on areas in which you lack talent and prevent you from developing strengths.

- You have a talent for noting people's progress and for helping them become even better at what they do. Look for a community service opportunity that lets you get "people done through work" rather than "work done through people."

- Consider getting involved in sports or intramural activities. You'll enjoy being part of a team and working with others toward a common goal.

- Your Developer talents will likely thrive in collaborative and people-oriented environments — where you can be part of a team but also have time to work one-on-one with others. Look for an after-school program that needs volunteers.

Discipline

Your world needs to be predictable. It needs to be ordered and planned. So you instinctively impose structure on your world. You set up routines. You focus on timelines and deadlines. You break long-term projects into a series of specific short-term plans, and you work through each plan diligently. You are not necessarily neat and clean, but you do need precision. Faced with the inherent messiness of life, you want to feel in control. The routines, the timelines, the structure, all of these help create this feeling of control. Lacking this theme of Discipline, others may sometimes resent your need for order, but there need not be conflict. You must understand that not everyone feels your urge for predictability; they have other ways of getting things done. Likewise, you can help them understand and even appreciate your need for structure. Your dislike of surprises, your impatience with errors, your routines and your detail orientation don't need to be misinterpreted as controlling behaviors that box people in. Rather, these behaviors can be understood as your instinctive method for maintaining your progress and your productivity in the face of life's many distractions.

Discipline Action Items

- How do you organize your day? You probably already have structures in place to ensure that you have everything under control. But when academic or social demands make you feel stressed or overwhelmed, consider breaking your daily to-do list into manageable sections, and leave yourself time to deal with the unexpected.

- If you are in a self-paced class or a class with minimal structure, develop your own structure to make sure that you meet the class requirements.

- What time of day are you most productive? When do you have the fewest distractions? You crave predictability and order. So when choosing courses, as much as possible, pick a routine class schedule, and make sure you will have time to study when you can focus on school.

- You are most effective when you can maintain order for yourself and others. Your talents for organization and structure can be useful in a wide variety of settings. Research internships that have controlled environments — that is where you will thrive.

- Detail all the steps of your career planning process, and follow them one by one. Put the steps on a timeline to keep you motivated. Share your plan with your academic adviser to help you keep the bigger picture in mind.

- Be the organizer for your friends. Offer to be the one who calls or texts everyone in your group to remind them about parties, class times, birthdays or future plans.

- Your powerful sense of order makes you a tremendous partner to those who need your Discipline talents to supplement their own. Build a complementary partnership with a friend or classmate who has talents where you don't. Being able to rely on each other and a mutual appreciation of each other's talents will strengthen your relationship.

- Organize a monthly or quarterly "clean up" day for you and your roommates. Try to make your living space look as good as it did on the day you moved in. Make it a party so it will be fun for everyone and something you can all look forward to.

- Exactitude is your forte; you enjoy poring over details. Save yourself from costly mistakes by scheduling time to go over all your financial documents — credit card charges, checking and savings account statements, financial aid records — to look for errors.

- You not only create order, but you crave it in the form of a well-organized space. To inspire your Discipline talents, find budget-friendly furniture and organization systems so you can have a place for everything and everything in its place.

- Increasing efficiency is one of your hallmarks. Do you ever feel like you might be wasting time or money because of your own or someone else's inefficiency? If so, identify those instances, and create systems to help you minimize waste and save time and money.

- You are a perfectionist at heart. Join a campus club where you can use your Discipline talents to help plan major events. You naturally break big tasks into smaller steps and focus on details and deadlines. Your Discipline talents help you keep everything under control so you can pull off important occasions smoothly.

- Is there a community service event that you can volunteer to help manage? Use your resourcefulness and organizational talents to help put people and money where they can do the most good.

Empathy

You can sense the emotions of those around you. You can feel what they are feeling as though their feelings are your own. Intuitively, you are able to see the world through their eyes and share their perspective. You do not necessarily agree with each person's perspective. You do not necessarily feel pity for each person's predicament — this would be sympathy, not Empathy. You do not necessarily condone the choices each person makes, but you do understand. This instinctive ability to understand is powerful. You hear the unvoiced questions. You anticipate the need. Where others grapple for words, you seem to find the right words and the right tone. You help people find the right phrases to express their feelings — to themselves as well as to others. You help them give voice to their emotional life. For all these reasons other people are drawn to you.

Empathy Action Items

- Keep a journal of everything you are feeling about your classes, friends and relationships with professors. When you reread what you wrote, ask yourself if you know what you are feeling is true, or if you are creating assumptions in your mind. Questioning and exploring your feelings can help you clarify them.

- Your Empathy talents are a valuable asset in student organizations or study groups. You are aware of what others are feeling and how they might react to different scenarios, and you may be the only one who is. To keep everyone moving toward the group's goals, give voice to what others are feeling, and bring emotions out into the open so you can clear the air and focus on the task ahead of you.

- When thinking about your major, consider fields that give you the chance to change lives. Your Empathy talents will likely make you successful in any area where you can have an impact on others. But roles that allow you to work with people one on one may be the most satisfying for you.

- Talk with a career counselor who can help you find internships or work environments that value emotions and do not repress them. A job with a rich emotional atmosphere will be the perfect setting for your Empathy talents.

- Be careful not to let those you support overwhelm you. You are there for your friends and family whenever they need you, but you also need to take care of yourself and find healthy ways to release your emotions. Discuss your feelings with your friends. They may not be as intuitive as you are, but they do care about you. So let them support you when you need it.

- Patience and understanding are the hallmarks of your talents. Be sure to hear your friends and roommates out; don't rush to judgment. Giving people time and space to sort out their own thoughts and feelings in a safe environment can foster their sense of stability and calm.

- You will sense when your friends are frustrated with school. Tell them that you know what they are feeling. Encourage them to write down or talk about their emotions, and see if any patterns emerge. Sometimes you're better at identifying and interpreting feelings than the person who's feeling them is. Give them some suggestions for coping based on what you hear.

- Seek out a mentor or friends with strong Analytical talents. They can help you see the rational side of a debate, discussion or situation — which you might miss when emotions are running high.

- You need to feel all of your feelings — good and bad. Avoid people who dismiss or disrespect this need.

- Become a confidante for one or two classmates or friends. Many college students feel overwhelmed. You have the natural talent to understand what they are going through. Be approachable. Tell them that you're happy to talk with them about what they are experiencing and feeling.

- The emotional tone of your environment might affect you more than it does other people. Because you are likely to feel the emotions of those around you as if they are your own, being around cheerful and upbeat people will make you feel optimistic as well. Find friends or roommates who have a lot of talent in the Positivity theme. Hanging out with them will make you feel good too.

- Interview people who are in campus organizations or clubs you are thinking about joining. When they talk about what they like or don't like, listen to how they describe their role, and notice their emotions and nonverbal communication. You will pick up on their passions and values, which will help you determine if the group is a fit for you.

- You can do a lot of good in the world — but be careful. Your Empathy talents may lead you to some very sad places: animal shelters, centers for the homeless, domestic abuse shelters. If you're an emotional sponge, it may be hard to shake off the sadness that comes with heartbreaking situations. The demands these feelings generate can distract you from your schoolwork and your own emotional health.

Focus

"Where am I headed?" you ask yourself. You ask this question every day. Guided by this theme of Focus, you need a clear destination. Lacking one, your life and your work can quickly become frustrating. And so each year, each month and even each week you set goals. These goals then serve as your compass, helping you determine priorities and make the necessary corrections to get back on course. Your Focus is powerful because it forces you to filter; you instinctively evaluate whether or not a particular action will help you move toward your goal. Those that don't are ignored. In the end, then, your Focus forces you to be efficient. Naturally, the flip side of this is that it causes you to become impatient with delays, obstacles and even tangents, no matter how intriguing they appear to be. This makes you an extremely valuable team member. When others start to wander down other avenues, you bring them back to the main road. Your Focus reminds everyone that if something is not helping you move toward your destination, then it is not important. And if it is not important, then it is not worth your time. You keep everyone on point.

Focus Action Items

- If you find yourself becoming too focused on your academic goals, stretch yourself to set personal goals. You are driven to achieve all your goals, and validating your personal priorities will bring a healthy balance to your life.

- What are your core values? Do the classes you are taking and your declared major align with your values? Will the career you choose fit with your life's purpose? Write down your beliefs, and refer to them often. Make sure not to ignore your beliefs as you chart your course to graduation and beyond. You will feel more in control of your life.

- As a person with strong Focus talents, you understand that life is about choices. Remember that your classmates, roommates and friends are responsible for making their own decisions. You might not agree with their choices or how they get there, but show them that you understand and respect their judgment. Or offer to help them if they have a hard time staying on track toward a goal.

- Set specific goals when planning your career. What do you want to achieve by the time you graduate? Pay attention to your destination and how you will get there. Your talent to stay on track is a powerful asset on your career journey.

- Although your Focus talents can reveal themselves through highly proactive goal setting, sometimes you might need someone else to identify a target for you. Find a classmate or mentor to help when the ultimate objective of an assignment or project is not clear to you.

- Make maintaining friendships one of your identifiable goals. Use your Focus talents to develop objectives that will enrich or broaden your social circle. Walk around your residence hall and on campus to catch up with old friends or meet new ones.

- Tell your roommate where you see yourself in the future. How do you set timelines and objectives that will help you achieve that vision? How can you help your roommate do the same thing?

- Many of your classmates will think, act and talk less efficiently than you do. Embrace these differences. Pay attention, and listen for opportunities in their "detours." They may send you down a path to new discoveries.

- Although you can easily concentrate for long periods of time, make sure to occasionally recharge yourself to avoid working to exhaustion. How often do you stop, get up and move around while you're studying? Taking a break every now and then will help you retain what you learn.

- To build on your Focus talents and not spread yourself too thin, be selective about how many activities you're involved in. What are your priorities? Identify someone in your support system who can help you see when things aren't balanced and pull you back on track.

- When you need to go to the gym, plan ahead. Ask a trainer when the gym is slowest, and work out then if you can. You won't have to wait around for other people to finish, and you'll find it easier to zero in on what you're doing.

- You like setting regular "mini goals" for yourself because they keep your Focus talents sharp. Create a daily goal to improve your health — walk with a friend, take a yoga class, try a healthy snack or go to bed 30 minutes earlier than usual.

- You may get frustrated with incomplete projects and groups that don't seem to get much done. So volunteer in organizations where you can contribute to a meaningful outcome with measurable results. Or find a leadership position in an organization you belong to already. You have the talents to make decisions for the group and to get stalled plans back on track.

Futuristic

"Wouldn't it be great if …" You are the kind of person who loves to peer over the horizon. The future fascinates you. As if it were projected on the wall, you see in detail what the future might hold, and this detailed picture keeps pulling you forward, into tomorrow. While the exact content of the picture will depend on your other strengths and interests — a better product, a better team, a better life or a better world — it will always be inspirational to you. You are a dreamer who sees visions of what could be and who cherishes those visions. When the present proves too frustrating and the people around you too pragmatic, you conjure up your visions of the future and they energize you. They can energize others too. In fact, very often people look to you to describe your visions of the future. They want a picture that can raise their sights and thereby their spirits. You can paint it for them. Practice. Choose your words carefully. Make the picture as vivid as possible. People will want to latch on to the hope you bring.

Futuristic Action Items

- You may be able to see and describe the future and what you will be doing, but you might not know exactly how to get there. Partner with someone who has strong Deliberative or Achiever talents to help you plan the steps you need to take to reach your vision.

- Apply your Futuristic talents to planning your life after college. Imagine yourself on graduation day. What are you doing? What experience, organizations and roles do you see on your résumé? Where are you headed after college — a new job, traveling the world or graduate school?

- Your natural ability to anticipate the future may mean you are not "in the present" to the extent you could be. Find friends who have powerful Adaptability, Context or Positivity talents. They can help you learn how to enjoy the moment.

- College is a great place to form authentic relationships that will last a lifetime. Surround yourself with people who align with your values, hopes and dreams. Take advantage of the wonderful opportunity to meet all kinds of people — some of whom may become a big part of your future.

- Because you can see what's coming, you should be prepared for it. Partner with friends or classmates who have Discipline or Arranger talents to help you organize your plans for the future. Someone with Activator, Discipline or Achiever can be instrumental when you need to stop planning and start working toward your goal.

- Work on the words you use to describe the future. Collaborate with friends or professors who have strong Communication, Ideation or Woo talents to find vivid visual images and stories that can persuade others to see the future's potential.

- Choose a major wisely by looking ahead. How in-demand will the careers in your field be in the next 10 or 20 years? Also, consider related academic minors and certificate programs. These additional study tracks can boost your employment opportunities, help your résumé stand out and give you some muscle when you're negotiating your salary.

- Even if you enjoy talking about possibilities more than problems, you may be able to help people see and prevent potential trouble. Maybe you can see that a friend's drinking habits are going to move from unwise to reckless to disastrous. Or your smart, hardworking roommate should aim for graduate school — but needs better financial habits to get there. Others will come to you for support because they trust what you see. Be sure to look ahead for your own obstacles as well.

- Use your Futuristic talents to break your preparation for final exams into smaller goals that you can accomplish weeks before the final test.

- Volunteer in an organization where you can help create the future by painting vivid pictures for those who work there. Help them see the role they will play in making the vision become reality.

- Join a group that believes it can have a positive effect on the future and that works toward its goal. Before you join, look at the mission statement to see if your values align with its purpose.

- You inspire your friends and classmates with your images of the future. When you articulate your vision, describe it in detail with vivid words and metaphors so that others can better comprehend your expansive thinking. Make your ideas and strategies more concrete using sketches, step-by-step action plans or mock-up models so that your peers can readily grasp your intent.

- When an organization, group or club needs to embrace change, use your Futuristic talents to help. Make a presentation or write an article that puts these changes in the context of the organization's future needs. You have a talent for putting things into perspective. And you can help others overcome their present uncertainties to become almost as excited as you are about the possibilities of the future.

Harmony

You look for areas of agreement. In your view there is little to be gained from conflict and friction, so you seek to hold them to a minimum. When you know that the people around you hold differing views, you try to find the common ground. You try to steer them away from confrontation and toward harmony. In fact, harmony is one of your guiding values. You can't quite believe how much time is wasted by people trying to impose their views on others. Wouldn't we all be more productive if we kept our opinions in check and instead looked for consensus and support? You believe we would, and you live by that belief. When others are sounding off about their goals, their claims and their fervently held opinions, you hold your peace. When others strike out in a direction, you will willingly, in the service of harmony, modify your own objectives to merge with theirs (as long as their basic values do not clash with yours). When others start to argue about their pet theory or concept, you steer clear of the debate, preferring to talk about practical, down-to-earth matters on which you can all agree. In your view we are all in the same boat, and we need this boat to get where we are going. It is a good boat. There is no need to rock it just to show that you can.

Harmony Action Items

- If you have professors who frequently change assignments and due dates, try to figure out their reasons — or ask them why they keep making changes. Then tell your classmates. Find the practical explanation, and give your professors the benefit of the doubt rather than complaining.

- Avoid confrontational, aggressive professors. They might make you so uncomfortable that learning in their classes will be difficult for you. Ask your academic adviser to help you find professors who will understand and respect how you learn.

- Polish your talent for resolution without agitation by acquiring skills and knowledge. Learn how to move through the steps of conflict resolution, and invite friends or classmates to learn with you. Encourage and inspire each other to become experts in finding solutions through consensus. By teaching others, you will learn as well.

- Your Harmony talents will flourish in collaborative environments in which you can surround yourself with others dedicated to win-win solutions. Look for internships where you can work with other students, professors or community members peacefully and positively toward a common goal.

- Try to explain to your friends and classmates the value of listening to all voices. Your attempts to create harmony by allowing everyone a turn to speak might actually create disharmony in some people. Individuals with exceptional Achiever or Activator talents, for example, may be eager to make a decision and take action.

- Look for friends or classmates who are especially talented in Command or Activator. When you have exhausted all your best efforts to resolve conflict, these people can help you deal with it head-on.

- When people in your classes or your residence hall are arguing or in an endless debate, help them find agreement. Create a trusting and respectful atmosphere so that everyone, especially quieter people, feels comfortable speaking their mind. Look for the practical side of things, and help others see it as well. It can be the starting point for agreement.

- Avoid classes, internships, extracurricular activities or jobs where you will have to confront people regularly. Sales roles that require cold calling or being in highly competitive environments or on aggressive teams, for example, are likely to frustrate or upset you.

- Use your Harmony talents to build a network of mentors with differing perspectives. Rely on these people when you need expertise. Your openness to their diverse views will help you learn.

- Your Harmony talents promote emotional stability in a group. This might be one reason your friends always invite you to go out with them — you know how to keep the peace so everyone can have a good time. Think through your budget before committing to plans, and don't feel bad about saying no if you can't afford to go out.

- Academic challenges can weigh heavily on your mind. When you are struggling, talk things through with friends you trust about the conflicts between your school commitments and your personal life. Ask them what they do when they're worried about school.

- If you're the leader on a team, find ways to unite everyone to be the best team you can be. You might enjoy helping team members get to know and appreciate one another. You have the talent to show others that they have more in common than they might first believe.

- Consider serving on a judicial board for a club or organization. You make people feel like they are truly being heard. That can have a big impact on other students' sense of engagement with your school.

Ideation

You are fascinated by ideas. What is an idea? An idea is a concept, the best explanation of the most events. You are delighted when you discover beneath the complex surface an elegantly simple concept to explain why things are the way they are. An idea is a connection. Yours is the kind of mind that is always looking for connections, and so you are intrigued when seemingly disparate phenomena can be linked by an obscure connection. An idea is a new perspective on familiar challenges. You revel in taking the world we all know and turning it around so we can view it from a strange but strangely enlightening angle. You love all these ideas because they are profound, because they are novel, because they are clarifying, because they are contrary, because they are bizarre. For all these reasons you derive a jolt of energy whenever a new idea occurs to you. Others may label you creative or original or conceptual or even smart. Perhaps you are all of these. Who can be sure? What you are sure of is that ideas are thrilling. And on most days this is enough.

Ideation Action Items

- Understand the fuel for your Ideation talents. When do you get your best ideas? When you're talking with classmates? When you're reading or studying? When you're simply listening or observing? Figure out the settings when you produce your best ideas, and re-create them as often as you can.

- If you get bored quickly, put your Ideation talents to work and think about how you can expand your world — your social network, your academic opportunities and your community involvement.

- Work with a professor to develop a research project that will require you to generate and explore numerous ideas. You love coming up with new ideas, and an innovative project can really boost your engagement. But be careful not to get so engrossed in the project that you work on it for hours without taking a break. Give your eyes and mind a rest. Go for a walk around campus — the change of pace will help you get out of your head so you can return to work fresh.

- Brainstorm with a career counselor about all the careers that could fit your talents. Check out the details of each career online, and then picture yourself in each one.

- Look for complementary partnerships on campus. A mentor with strong Analytical talents will have the objectivity to challenge your big ideas and will support you to explore them further. Classmates and friends who have strong Intellection, Maximizer or Achiever talents can help you harness all your ideas and turn the best ones into reality. You can be their inspiration; they can help you realize your dreams.

- Find other students or professors who have different viewpoints and backgrounds than you do and who like to talk about their ideas. Their fascinating — at least to you — perspective can inspire you. By feeding one another's need for big thinking, you can build mutually supportive and satisfying relationships.

- What new concepts are you excited about? Share your ideas with your roommates, friends, classmates or family. Ideating with them will help them understand you better and can really let them see the core of what you love, value and are passionate about.

- How could you use your creativity to help improve your fraternity or sorority, residence hall, or campus? First, see the idea, and then find others to help you accomplish what you see. Have a brainstorming party with your friends and roommates to come up with a plan. Working together is a fun way to make your college environment better and grow your relationships.

- Choose classes that involve creative projects rather than just exams and term papers. You will love generating ideas, but sometimes you may struggle with implementing them. Find a partner with strong Responsibility talents who can keep you on a work schedule and help you meet deadlines.

- Help revive a struggling group on campus. You will probably have lots of opinions and thoughts on how to bring it back to life. Or consider starting a new group with other big thinkers, and generate ideas about projects to engage the team.

- Volunteer in organizations where leaders encourage and solicit your divergent thinking. You can come up with new and better strategies for the organization, and you may be able to help in its planning meetings. Persuading leaders to consider new approaches may lead to future career opportunities as well.

- You are a natural fit with research and development; you appreciate the mindset of visionaries and dreamers. Feed your Ideation talents by spending time with your imaginative peers. Sit in on their brainstorming sessions. Which of their clubs or organizations sound most appealing to you?

- Find classes, clubs or projects that align with your interests and areas of passion. Look for groups where you can use your creative talents. An organization that sticks to traditions and resists innovation may feel stifling to you.

Includer

"Stretch the circle wider." This is the philosophy around which you orient your life. You want to include people and make them feel part of the group. In direct contrast to those who are drawn only to exclusive groups, you actively avoid those groups that exclude others. You want to expand the group so that as many people as possible can benefit from its support. You hate the sight of someone on the outside looking in. You want to draw them in so that they can feel the warmth of the group. You are an instinctively accepting person. Regardless of race or sex or nationality or personality or faith, you cast few judgments. Judgments can hurt a person's feelings. Why do that if you don't have to? Your accepting nature does not necessarily rest on a belief that each of us is different and that one should respect these differences. Rather, it rests on your conviction that fundamentally we are all the same. We are all equally important. Thus, no one should be ignored. Each of us should be included. It is the least we all deserve.

Includer Action Items

- Form a study group with your classmates. If some people in the group do not talk very often, invite them to participate in the discussion. You naturally know how to make everyone feel respected and like they belong.

- Attend lectures or presentations featuring guest speakers of different nationalities. Introduce yourself to others attending the session, and encourage them to join in a conversation.

- Sign up for classes in which you will study particular groups of people, like sociology or anthropology. You will enjoy learning about diverse cultures and backgrounds, and you will naturally notice what they have in common. Use what you learn to help your friends and classmates understand that to respect all the differences among people, they must first appreciate all the similarities.

- Welcome new students to your residence hall. Be a first friend. Get to know their names, and introduce them to other students. You will make many friends this way. It's hard to forget the person who first made you feel like you belonged in a new place.

- Be an "Includer coach" for your friends and roommates. Some people may require a caring nudge to get them to step outside their comfort zone and add someone to their inner circle. Help them understand that when they leave others out, they might miss the chance for an important future relationship.

- Take the initiative in planning a group event or activity for your residence hall. You enjoy connecting people who wouldn't typically get together.

- In some situations, more doesn't mean better. That can be hard for you to accept. When planning an intimate get-together, you may need help drawing limits when you can't include everyone. Sometimes it is OK not to invite everybody. Partner with a friend who has strong Command talents to help you decide on the final guest list.

- You will be most comfortable in open, welcoming environments. You may prefer going to an easygoing and relaxed fitness class versus an intense boot camp full of competitive individual achievers. Ask around campus to find fun, nonjudgmental fitness classes, and encourage your friends to go with you.

- Your friendliness and approachability can unite groups and teams. Consider signing up for an intramural sport to participate in this semester. Find classmates and friends to join with you.

- Which professors, students or community leaders do you admire for their ability to accept others without judgment? Talk with them about the need for tolerance for all people. These experienced Includers can inspire and expand your talents.

- Your Includer talents will flourish in positions where you can welcome others. College is a great place to meet new students and put them at ease. Volunteer to be an orientation leader, a greeter in your residence hall — or consider joining a welcoming committee on campus.

- Do you enjoy speaking up for unheard voices? Look for organizations in your community that welcome and advocate for people who might not have many social or economic privileges. Empower your Includer talents by volunteering or tutoring at these organizations.

- Develop or participate in programs that promote diversity. You can make a big difference by raising awareness and welcoming all kinds of people. Invite friends who you think could expand or enrich the program.

Individualization

Your Individualization theme leads you to be intrigued by the unique qualities of each person. You are impatient with generalizations or "types" because you don't want to obscure what is special and distinct about each person. Instead, you focus on the differences between individuals. You instinctively observe each person's style, each person's motivation, how each thinks and how each builds relationships. You hear the one-of-a-kind stories in each person's life. This theme explains why you pick your friends just the right birthday gift, why you know that one person prefers praise in public and another detests it, and why you tailor your teaching style to accommodate one person's need to be shown and another's desire to "figure it out as I go." Because you are such a keen observer of other people's strengths, you can draw out the best in each person. This Individualization theme also helps you build productive teams. While some search around for the perfect team "structure" or "process," you know instinctively that the secret to great teams is casting by individual strengths so that everyone can do a lot of what they do well.

Individualization Action Items

- Establish a study group with classmates who have a wide variety of talents and perspectives. Learning about different personalities and viewpoints will expand your own horizons.

- Pay attention to how your style of learning, studying, writing papers and taking tests compares with others'. What are some of the differences you see? Are your friends and classmates doing anything that might help you in your studies? Collaborate on the best ways to tackle assignments and projects using everyone's input.

- You want to have the best fit between who you are and what you do with your life. Go to the career center and explore different professions that interest you. To guide your decision, think about how the various career options offer you a unique picture of yourself.

- Interview teachers, counselors, HR reps, coaches, doctors and others who are paid to see the uniqueness in people. How do they use their talents in their career?

- You can learn a lot from your boss no matter what kind of job you have. Where others might see an authority figure who tells them what to do, your Individualization talents let you see a person with unique responsibilities and talents. Use what you observe in your work environment now to determine what kind of boss you want to have — or be — after graduation.

- Tell your friends and roommates about the great talents you see in them, and encourage them to follow their dreams. Help them understand and maximize the power of their unique strengths, and help them find or create experiences and opportunities to shine.

- Become an expert at describing your own strengths and style. Then organize a get-together in your residence hall, fraternity or sorority. Use what you learned about yourself to explore the individuality of everyone who shows up. Starting with strengths is a great way to get to know the people you spend a lot of time with and to stimulate conversations about their future plans.

- Constantly observe those around you. How do you spot what others do well and how they are each unique? Appreciate how the nuances in talents highlight similarities and differences.

- How do you respond when your peers don't notice the unique contributions you make to a class, project or relationship? How can you help them see more of the layers that make you unique? Try telling them what you see that makes them special. When you acknowledge their talents, they might also start to recognize and appreciate your talents and contributions.

- You move comfortably among a broad range of styles and cultures, and you intuitively personalize your interactions. Make full use of these talents by leading diversity efforts on campus and in the community.

- Consider keeping a journal of specific observations you make about individual students or professors. Then share your observations so everyone on campus can see what these individuals uniquely bring to your school. Write feature articles about them for the school newspaper or college newsletter. Or create a blog or podcast that highlights their contributions.

- Volunteer to help with the pledging process for a fraternity or sorority. Your Individualization talents are valuable on search committees and in recruiting processes because you can see how each individual's talents fit particular roles.

- Environments that let you work one on one with people and focus on individual performance may bring out your best. Look for volunteer or work-study opportunities where you can mentor others or provide feedback. They could open the door to future career prospects.

Input

You are inquisitive. You collect things. You might collect information — words, facts, books and quotations — or you might collect tangible objects such as butterflies, baseball cards, porcelain dolls or sepia photographs. Whatever you collect, you collect it because it interests you. And yours is the kind of mind that finds so many things interesting. The world is exciting precisely because of its infinite variety and complexity. If you read a great deal, it is not necessarily to refine your theories but, rather, to add more information to your archives. If you like to travel, it is because each new location offers novel artifacts and facts. These can be acquired and then stored away. Why are they worth storing? At the time of storing it is often hard to say exactly when or why you might need them, but who knows when they might become useful? With all those possible uses in mind, you really don't feel comfortable throwing anything away. So you keep acquiring and compiling and filing stuff away. It's interesting. It keeps your mind fresh. And perhaps one day some of it will prove valuable.

Input Action Items

- Identify areas of specialization within your major, and actively pursue more information about them. Connect with faculty who work in those areas, and pick their brains outside of class.

- You are naturally curious, but you may need to intentionally schedule time to feed your mind. Read books and articles that stimulate you, or travel to new places. Take the time you need to sustain your Input talents.

- What is your learning style? You may like collecting information through reading, through people, through listening or through doing. Have an answer to this question when you meet with your academic adviser to enroll in classes for the next semester — and try to get into classes that fit with your style.

- Knowing when to stop digging is just as valuable as your thirst for information. Set a time limit on your internet searches so you will be able to get your schoolwork done. Mark the best sites so you can return to them when you have free time.

- How can you prioritize the most important information to study in your classes? Take notes and collaborate with other students to see if they noted the same information you did. This is a good way to make sure you aren't distracted by material that fascinates you but is not as relevant to the course.

- Your mind is like a sponge; you naturally soak up information. But just as a sponge does not permanently contain what it absorbs, your mind shouldn't simply store information. Input without output can lead to stagnation. As you gather information, ask yourself which of your friends or classmates could benefit from what you learned, and then share it with them.

- Seek out a mentor with Focus or Discipline talents who can help channel your interests productively and organize everything you've discovered so that the information is easily accessible for you.

- Use your Input talents to help others. When a friend has an issue, volunteer to learn more about it. If a family member has a health concern, research it online, and help them think of insightful questions they can ask at their next doctor's appointment.

- When you meet other students in your classes or residence hall who share your interests, think beyond the immediate connection. Use your Input talents as a stepping stone to friendship. When you hear about upcoming events that coincide with your common interests — a music festival or a guest speaker on campus — invite these people to go with you.

- Your mind never stops, and you love to contemplate, read and explore. But sometimes, that can make sleep a challenge. Create a system to ensure that you are getting the proper amount of sleep. For example, use your Input talents to research the best ways to get a good night's sleep, how to set up an effective sleep schedule or how to wind down before bedtime.

- You are extremely resourceful. This is a big advantage when forming a team. Since you "collect" the strengths and talents of those around you, you know how to place people where they can be at their best. Whatever organization you are in, make it stronger by investing in team and group development.

- Get as much information as you can about community service opportunities that interest you. Research online, attend career fairs and collect all the brochures you can find. The more information you gather, the better your decisions will be.

- Other students might see you as a leader because they know you are resourceful and aware of recent developments and information. Let people know that you enjoy answering their questions and researching their pressing issues. Use your Input talents to connect with classmates, and look for a leadership role on campus where you can use what you collect.

Intellection

You like to think. You like mental activity. You like exercising the "muscles" of your brain, stretching them in multiple directions. This need for mental activity may be focused; for example, you may be trying to solve a problem or develop an idea or understand another person's feelings. The exact focus will depend on your other strengths. On the other hand, this mental activity may very well lack focus. The theme of Intellection does not dictate what you are thinking about; it simply describes that you like to think. You are the kind of person who enjoys your time alone because it is your time for musing and reflection. You are introspective. In a sense you are your own best companion, as you pose yourself questions and try out answers on yourself to see how they sound. This introspection may lead you to a slight sense of discontent as you compare what you are actually doing with all the thoughts and ideas that your mind conceives. Or this introspection may tend toward more pragmatic matters such as the events of the day or a conversation that you plan to have later. Wherever it leads you, this mental hum is one of the constants of your life.

Intellection Action Items

- You think up great questions, and you enjoy asking them. Use that gift to ask yourself some questions. When have you felt best about your accomplishments? What did you do to contribute to those accomplishments? How have you used your talents successfully? Your intense self-examination will make you a stronger and more confident student.

- When do you do your best thinking — alone or with others, in a quiet environment or a noisy one, while in motion or sitting still? Find your best atmosphere to think, and make sure that you give yourself all the time you need to reflect.

- Follow your intellectual curiosity, and allow yourself to ask the questions that naturally come to you. This will help you refine your approach to learning and studying.

- Keep a journal, and record your thoughts regularly. Your ideas will serve as grist for your mental mill, and they might yield valuable insights. Writing might be the best way to crystallize and integrate your thoughts.

- Research careers that interest you by reading biographies of people in those careers and collecting brochures in the career center. Reading will give you clarity about the career options that fit you best. Talk through your thoughts with your friends to process what you have learned.

- The energetic debate of a philosophical issue can sometimes intimidate those with lesser Intellection talents. Partner with someone who has strong Empathy or Positivity talents to help you recognize the signs of others' discomfort when discussions become intense.

- Some people will want you to think with them, while others will want you to think for them. You build complementary relationships with some people because you look at things from an entirely different angle than they do. Become a thinking partner for your determined and action-oriented friends; you may be the sounding board they need to improve their odds for success.

- Form relationships with other students and classmates you consider to be big thinkers. How can they inspire you to focus your own thinking?

- Remember that other people cannot read your mind. Practice putting your thoughts into words so your classmates can better understand what you are thinking. Give them a glimpse into what is happening inside your head by translating your ideas into language they can relate to, and allow them time to process and ask questions.

- Help your friends and roommates understand that your need for solitude and space to think has a positive impact on your mental health and is simply your intellectual style. Let them know that you are not ignoring or avoiding them, but that you want to bring your best to school and relationships — and to do that, you need time alone to think.

- You are at your best when you have the time to follow an intellectual trail and see where it leads. Others will seek out your opinion because they appreciate your careful scrutiny. Get involved on the public side of community service projects, campus events and extracurricular activities so that your thinking can have a greater impact on long-term outcomes.

- What do you find intellectually inspiring? What big ideas would you like to ponder or discuss? Consider writing for your college's blog to stimulate your thinking. Use your natural desire to contemplate and muse to engage other students in class or study group discussions about global topics that are important to your campus, your generation and your future.

- Find other students who like to talk about the same issues you do. Organize a discussion group that addresses your subjects of interest. Encourage people in the group to use their full intellectual capital by reframing questions and engaging them in dialogue.

Learner

You love to learn. The subject matter that interests you most will be determined by your other themes and experiences, but whatever the subject, you will always be drawn to the process of learning. The process, more than the content or the result, is especially exciting for you. You are energized by the steady and deliberate journey from ignorance to competence. The thrill of the first few facts, the early efforts to recite or practice what you have learned, the growing confidence of a skill mastered — this is the process that entices you. Your excitement leads you to engage in adult learning experiences — yoga or piano lessons or graduate classes. It enables you to thrive in dynamic work environments where you are asked to take on short project assignments and are expected to learn a lot about the new subject matter in a short period of time and then move on to the next one. This Learner theme does not necessarily mean that you seek to become the subject matter expert, or that you are striving for the respect that accompanies a professional or academic credential. The outcome of the learning is less significant than the "getting there."

Learner Action Items

- You love the challenge of a steep learning curve, so beware of learning plateaus. Look for opportunities to stretch yourself by volunteering for complex class assignments or taking difficult courses.

- Use your talents to learn about yourself. Identify your learning style. Monitor your progress toward meeting your requirements for graduation. Pay attention to how you change and grow while you are in college. You naturally love to learn, and what better topic to learn about than yourself?

- Find ways to track your learning progress to keep yourself motivated. If there are distinct levels of learning in your classes or specific milestones toward earning your degree, celebrate your progression from one stage to the next. If there aren't any specific steps, create them for yourself.

- Learning is meaningful to you, and it always will be. Remember that you will never stop learning, even when school is over. Keep a journal of your college experiences now so that when you are older, you can look back and remember all the lessons you learned.

- You love the process of learning so much that the outcome may not matter to you. As a result, you might have a number of unfinished projects that you plan to come back to "someday." Partner with classmates or friends with strong Activator, Focus or Achiever talents who can help you complete those projects and become even more productive and purposeful in your education.

- Become an expert in an area that interests you — academics, sports, performance arts — to feed your need for extreme competency. Set goals so that you know when you've reached the level of a master or expert. Use your mastery to mentor friends or classmates who are interested in learning about your area of expertise.

- Be a catalyst for change. Some people are intimidated by new rules or new skills — but they might still need to learn them for a class or to keep moving forward. Apply your willingness to soak up newness to calm their fears and spur them into action.

- Go online and search for upcoming events on campus. Look for workshops on money management or speakers who discuss healthy lifestyle changes. Look to the wider community if you can't find anything on campus. You will enjoy hearing and learning about a variety of different topics.

- When you are immersed in studying and concentrating intensely on your subject, you might lose track of time. To allow yourself the time you want and need, schedule study sessions when you have the fewest interruptions.

Having a set schedule and enough time to study can give you confidence and reduce your test anxiety.

- Honor your desire to learn. Take advantage of your campus resources, and consider trying something new. You might have more options than you realize — many schools have an array of different groups, clubs and intramural sports. Set a goal to sign up for a least one new extracurricular activity each year.

- How do you learn best and feel most connected to the space around you? If you learn through teaching, find opportunities to give presentations on campus. If you learn by doing, look for workshops that teach skills or crafts. If you learn best through silent reflection, find areas around campus that are good meditation spots.

- Collaborate with faculty or become a teaching assistant to make your college experience more meaningful. Teaching others will deepen your understanding of and appreciation for intellectual topics, concepts and principles.

- Get involved. Join a fraternity, sorority, choir, campus organization, residence hall leadership team or another university club. You will love learning about the people, traditions and goals of the group, and your Learner talents will make you a vital part of any team you belong to.

Maximizer

Excellence, not average, is your measure. Taking something from below average to slightly above average takes a great deal of effort and in your opinion is not very rewarding. Transforming something strong into something superb takes just as much effort but is much more thrilling. Strengths, whether yours or someone else's, fascinate you. Like a diver after pearls, you search them out, watching for the telltale signs of a strength. A glimpse of untutored excellence, rapid learning, a skill mastered without recourse to steps — all these are clues that a strength may be in play. And having found a strength, you feel compelled to nurture it, refine it and stretch it toward excellence. You polish the pearl until it shines. This natural sorting of strengths means that others see you as discriminating. You choose to spend time with people who appreciate your particular strengths. Likewise, you are attracted to others who seem to have found and cultivated their own strengths. You tend to avoid those who want to fix you and make you well-rounded. You don't want to spend your life bemoaning what you lack. Rather, you want to capitalize on the gifts with which you are blessed. It's more fun. It's more productive. And, counterintuitively, it is more demanding.

Maximizer Action Items

- Choose your major based on your greatest talents and your personal mission. Find specialized programs in your area of interest where you can use your talents and fulfill your developmental goals.

- Spending a lot of time in an area where you are not strong will frustrate and drain you. So make your weaknesses irrelevant as much as you can. For example, if you have required classes in a subject you are struggling with, find friends or classmates who are good at it, and partner with them. Or devise a support system — join a study group or find a tutor. Or figure out how to use your stronger talents to compensate for your weaker areas.

- Interview people who are among the best of the best in jobs that interest you. Ask them what they find most rewarding about their work. Job shadow them to see what they do day in and day out. Pay attention to the talents, knowledge and skills that excellence in those roles requires.

- Are there parts of your life that could use improvement? What can you do to make them better? What can you take from strong to superb? Refine your talents and skills, and define what excellence means to you. Figure out how to measure your progress.

- You naturally focus on things that other people can improve on, yet sometimes you can become distracted from your own development. Look for a mentor who will focus on your strengths. Meet regularly with your mentor and other role models for insight, advice and inspiration on how you can go from good to great.

- You love to help others become excited by their potential, and you naturally see what people do best. If your college has a mentorship program for incoming freshmen, sign up to be a mentor. Or find programs in your community that give you the opportunity to coach or tutor. You see glimpses of excellence and can help new students start on the right foot to developing their strengths.

- Problem-solving might drain your energy and enthusiasm. Just as you are probably aware of what you do well, you know when you need help. Look for friends with strong Restorative talents who can help you troubleshoot and resolve complex and confusing issues. Let them know how important their partnership is to your success.

- Explain to your friends and roommates why you don't spend a lot of time trying to fix problems.

People who don't know you well might confuse your Maximizer talents with arrogance or think you don't care. Help them understand that endless difficulties and complications can sap your energy, and you are much better at noticing what is working and making the most of it.

- Keep your focus on long-term relationships and goals. Many people pick the low-hanging fruit of short-term success, but your Maximizer talents will be most energized and effective when you can turn potential into true and lasting greatness.

- During your school's activity fair, look for a club or organization that gives you the opportunity to improve your health, meet new friends and boost your engagement on campus. You will enjoy making the most of the time you spend in your extracurricular activities.

- Ask around your residence hall to find groups, clubs or teams you can join that do great work and have high levels of performance. Belonging to a group where members "just show up" won't be a good experience for you because you need to be part of something excellent that matters to you.

- Take on a leadership role that aligns with your personal mission. You know that talent is every team's greatest resource, so get the highest return on your investment of that resource. Use your Maximizer talents to help group members see their own talents, and then position people where they can best develop and apply their strengths. For every need, there is a person with a gift to match.

- Study success. Spend time with people who have discovered and use their strengths. Do you have any professors who are clearly doing what they do best — and who make it look easy? Talk with them about the power of their talents and strengths. The more you understand how using strengths leads to success, the more likely you will be to create success in your own life.

Positivity

You are generous with praise, quick to smile and always on the lookout for the positive in the situation. Some call you lighthearted. Others just wish that their glass were as full as yours seems to be. But either way, people want to be around you. Their world looks better around you because your enthusiasm is contagious. Lacking your energy and optimism, some find their world drab with repetition or, worse, heavy with pressure. You seem to find a way to lighten their spirit. You inject drama into every project. You celebrate every achievement. You find ways to make everything more exciting and more vital. Some cynics may reject your energy, but you are rarely dragged down. Your Positivity won't allow it. Somehow you can't quite escape your conviction that it is good to be alive, that work can be fun and that no matter what the setbacks, one must never lose one's sense of humor.

Positivity Action Items

- Meet with your academic adviser to help you select courses taught by professors who have affirming teaching styles. Your classes need to be exciting and meaningful. Connect with your peers who also have strong Positivity talents to see what they say about the courses you are considering.

- Use your naturally optimistic outlook to give your friends and roommates a boost. You will be able to tell when they are feeling overwhelmed or tense about school, money, work or relationships. When your friends need a break, plan a hike or a weekend camping trip. Spending time outdoors can help reduce stress.

- Invite your upbeat friends and classmates to study with you. Together, think of fun, even trivial, ways to remember critical information.

- Choose friends who love life as much as you do. Let positive emotions reign, and avoid those who have negative, destructive and defeating attitudes and behaviors.

- Because of your optimism, you can accept solutions that are less than ideal. As a result, you encourage yourself and others to make progress rather than insisting on perfection. Find a mentor with strong Maximizer talents to help you look for and describe the potential in less-than-ideal situations. Encourage yourself to take risks to improve, even when you don't have the total solution yet.

- You may be one of the few bright spots in someone's life — especially if they're going through a difficult time. Never underestimate that role. People will come to you because they know they can count on you to raise their spirits. When they do, be ready to ask questions so that you can easily identify what they need most from you.

- As much as you value positive friends and people, you value authentic friendships even more. Be true to your moods, and recognize your friends' vulnerability. Acknowledge your own and others' sadness and fear, and help put feelings into words.

- Make sure that your praise is always genuine — never empty or false. False praise can be more damaging than criticism. If you believe it, say it. If you don't, show your respect for others' intelligence, and don't give in to false flattery. Authentic actions will help you build long-lasting genuine relationships.

- Your energy and optimism are contagious, and your friends appreciate the vibe you bring to all your social gatherings. Look for activities on or off campus that are free or offer a student discount, and invite your friends to a fun outing where you can relax and blow off steam.

- When people feel better, they often perform better. Sometimes feelings are the result of action; other times, feelings are the cause for action. Find reasons to celebrate, laugh, and inject music and joy into your friends' lives. A positive emotional environment will help everyone do better in their classes, particularly during tense times like finals week.

- Play sports or support your school's teams by cheering them on. What sports are your friends involved in? What team doesn't have many fans and needs more of your positive mojo? Consider supporting the school's bowling team — what better place to be a fan than a bowling alley, with fun music and a snack bar.

- You excel in roles in which you can highlight the positive. A leadership position will capitalize on your ability to make things dramatic. Get involved in a club or group that needs an optimistic leader who can motivate others through fun, energy and excitement about the group's goals.

- Look for opportunities to help plan celebrations for your family, campus or community. You have the ability to turn small achievements into memorable events, and people look forward to your parties.

- Avoid cynical and negative environments and people. They will drain you. As much as possible, look for relaxed classes and clubs that will appreciate your optimism and sense of humor.

Relator

Relator describes your attitude toward your relationships. In simple terms, the Relator theme pulls you toward people you already know. You do not necessarily shy away from meeting new people — in fact, you may have other themes that cause you to enjoy the thrill of turning strangers into friends — but you do derive a great deal of pleasure and strength from being around your close friends. You are comfortable with intimacy. Once the initial connection has been made, you deliberately encourage a deepening of the relationship. You want to understand their feelings, their goals, their fears and their dreams; and you want them to understand yours. You know that this kind of closeness implies a certain amount of risk — you might be taken advantage of — but you are willing to accept that risk. For you a relationship has value only if it is genuine. And the only way to know that is to entrust yourself to the other person. The more you share with each other, the more you risk together. The more you risk together, the more each of you proves your caring is genuine. These are your steps toward real friendship, and you take them willingly.

Relator Action Items

- Share your academic progress and performance with people who care about you at school and at home. By opening up to others, you encourage them to be open and honest with you, which will deepen your friendship.

- Choose courses that your friends are taking. Having friends in class will increase your engagement throughout the semester.

- Talk to your trusted circle of friends about how they see you. Ask them what they think your greatest talents are. You value and trust your best friends' opinions, and they can give you a new perspective on yourself. Keep in mind how others perceive you when you go to class, socialize, volunteer — and even when you graduate and start your future career.

- You may not enjoy jobs that require you to be alone a lot. Your Relator talents shine when you are around people, so a part-time job that pays a little more may not be worth it if it keeps you solitary. Instead, look for a job where you can connect with people and potentially form close friendships with your coworkers.

- How much one-on-one time are you getting with the key people in your life? Make sure you have the dedicated time and emotional energy to share with those who are closest to you. Don't let the demands of college and other commitments make you miss opportunities to show your friends that you care. A genuine friendship will endure over time.

- Establish various lines of communication with friends in your classes — verbal, text, email — and help each other with lectures, notes and assignments when one of you has to miss class.

- Get to know the professors, counselors and advisers who take an interest in you. Their involvement in your college experience will help you feel like you belong and stimulate your intellectual development as well as your academic achievement.

- As a strong Relator, you may get and give more love and friendship than most. Tell people that your relationship with them makes you happy. Show them that you care about the quality of their lives by extending compassion, thoughtfulness and interest in their core values.

- Be a mentor, and find a mentor. You enjoy learning about the people you meet, understanding them and forming genuine bonds. So as a mentor, you will offer sincere and caring guidance. And when you are looking for a mentor, consider someone with strong Belief talents who can help you connect with others based on common values.

- You are a giver, not a taker. But sometimes, you need to recharge your own battery. Identify close friends you can trust and open up to during troubling times, and lean on them for the support you need. To have the energy to help others who look to you for deep and genuine friendship, you have to take care of your needs first.

- Consider doing justice-based and humanitarian work that you can rally your close friends to be a part of as well. You will strengthen your friendships by working together toward a meaningful common goal.

- Try to socialize outside of your classes or regular group or club meetings sometimes. Meet new friends for lunch or coffee, or walk to class together. You might find opportunities for lasting relationships when you look outside your comfort zone.

- Research prospective groups before you agree to volunteer to their cause. You will not do well in an overly formal environment that discourages friendships. Find out what an organization's culture is like before you commit to joining. Remember this when you choose a career as well. Look for company cultures that value in-depth, meaningful relationships.

Responsibility

Your Responsibility theme forces you to take psychological ownership for anything you commit to, and whether large or small, you feel emotionally bound to follow it through to completion. Your good name depends on it. If for some reason you cannot deliver, you automatically start to look for ways to make it up to the other person. Apologies are not enough. Excuses and rationalizations are totally unacceptable. You will not quite be able to live with yourself until you have made restitution. This conscientiousness, this near obsession for doing things right, and your impeccable ethics, combine to create your reputation: utterly dependable. When assigning new responsibilities, people will look to you first because they know it will get done. When people come to you for help — and they soon will — you must be selective. Your willingness to volunteer may sometimes lead you to take on more than you should.

Responsibility Action Items

- What does it mean to be a responsible college student? Make a list of times in the past when your hard work and commitments in school paid off and made you successful. Use your past academic achievement to create a standard for yourself, and work toward it gradually, one step at a time. Your Responsibility talents will prompt you to fulfill what you promised yourself you would do.

- Make an appointment with a career counselor to talk about how to begin planning for your career. The resulting sense of psychological ownership will engage you in the process and energize you to follow through.

- You thrive in environments that focus on outcomes. Explore different internships that emphasize and reward results over processes and procedures.

- Ask your friends and family what "doing the right thing" means to them. You might be surprised at their answers, which will reveal glimmers of their talents. You'll also hear the unspoken assumptions and expectations people have of you, which is invaluable because you never want to let anyone down.

- Develop partnerships with friends or classmates who have strong Relator talents. They can point out when your commitments are causing you to neglect those who mean the most to you.

- You win others over by following through with your commitments. People rely on you because they know you will complete a project — and do it right. Volunteer to be the one in your study group, fraternity or sorority, or residence hall to take ownership for quality and for making sure your group's initiatives get done on time and on budget.

- Find mentors or classmates who have powerful Positivity talents. These partners can help you lighten up when you feel like you have the weight of the world on your shoulders.

- Look for classmates or people in your residence hall who also have the Responsibility theme in their top five. You will flourish in relationships with friends who share your determination to get things done.

- Find a workout buddy who is especially talented in Discipline or Focus. This person can help you stay on track with your exercise routine and prevent you from becoming overloaded with other commitments.

- Have you considered running for student government? You may feel that if you *can* make things better, you *should* make things better. Student government is a good way to improve your whole school. But it is also a huge time commitment. If you run, make sure that you have enough time to give it your all — without hurting your other responsibilities or your personal life.

- Students who don't have strong Responsibility talents might be difficult for you to cope with; you may feel like they don't take school as seriously as they should. But remember, everyone has strengths that a group needs. People with Harmony talents may skip class or your study group meetings, but when they do show up, you get more done with less conflict.

- Keep in mind that you can help others while still keeping the promises you have made to yourself. Your personal commitments are no less important than your friends' requests for help. Give yourself permission to say no sometimes.

- Figure out how much time you can realistically devote to clubs and activities and what your priorities are. Saying yes too quickly when new opportunities come your way might mean you have to say no to something else.

- Building trusting relationships with others is important to you, so choose environments in which you can surround yourself with dependable, trustworthy people. When selecting a team to join, be sure the other members will uphold their end to ensure the team's success.

Restorative

You love to solve problems. Whereas some are dismayed when they encounter yet another breakdown, you can be energized by it. You enjoy the challenge of analyzing the symptoms, identifying what is wrong and finding the solution. You may prefer practical problems or conceptual ones or personal ones. You may seek out specific kinds of problems that you have met many times before and that you are confident you can fix. Or you may feel the greatest push when faced with complex and unfamiliar problems. Your exact preferences are determined by your other themes and experiences. But what is certain is that you enjoy bringing things back to life. It is a wonderful feeling to identify the undermining factor(s), eradicate them and restore something to its true glory. Intuitively, you know that without your intervention, this thing — this machine, this technique, this person, this company — might have ceased to function. You fixed it, resuscitated it, rekindled its vitality. Phrasing it the way you might, you saved it.

Restorative Action Items

- Think about school as a way to improve yourself. Cultivating your skills and knowledge might increase your motivation to find solutions, particularly when you reflect on your progress.

- When you get a test back, review the questions you missed. Try studying every test question you didn't answer correctly to determine recurring gaps in your knowledge. Then figure out how to fix the problem. But don't get so focused on what was wrong that you forget to celebrate the questions you got right.

- Diagnosing problems and designing solutions can make your Restorative talents flourish. Meet with your academic adviser to find courses or internships that require troubleshooting and analysis.

- If you had the opportunity to change one thing for the better, what would it be and how would you go about changing it? Share this thought-provoking question with your friends, professors and classmates.

- Ask faculty and staff if there are any lost university traditions that would benefit your school now. Consider having an alumni reunion to learn about the customs or rituals of your college that have disappeared — and why. How could you bring them back to life for today's students?

- Be careful not to get stuck focusing on what's wrong with your relationships. Make sure your friends and roommates don't think that flaws and shortcomings are all you can see.

- Do your friends and family know about your passion for working through problems? If not, tell them. Offer to help them think through their difficulties. Your natural ability to fix problems is not natural for everyone. You might be a powerful partner they didn't even know they had.

- Your strong Restorative talents might make you overly critical of yourself sometimes. Give yourself a break. When you get frustrated trying to solve a problem, look for a mentor or friends with strong Ideation talents. These partners can add an element of creativity and help you think of other ways to handle a stressful situation.

- Use your Restorative talents not only to tackle existing problems but also to anticipate and prevent problems before they occur. For example, share your foresight and your solutions for potential student debt issues with your roommates and friends. You will prove yourself to be a valuable partner.

- Turnaround situations activate your natural forte. Use your Restorative talents to devise a plan of attack to revitalize your own or a friend's health by researching nutritious diets and developing a workout plan.

- You define yourself by your ability to cope, but if you can't solve a particular problem, don't feel defeated. Look to your support system to help you through roadblocks, and explore counseling services on campus.

- Volunteer with an organization that needs someone to breathe new life into its work. Intervening and restoring vitality is what you do best.

- Consider getting involved in local revitalization projects. Many communities have neighborhood improvement associations that work with local governments and universities to improve historical districts. They need researchers, carpenters, historians, fundraisers, college liaisons — a host of roles that would allow you to apply your talents on a larger scale.

Self-Assurance

Self-Assurance is similar to self-confidence. In the deepest part of you, you have faith in your strengths. You know that you are able — able to take risks, able to meet new challenges, able to stake claims and, most important, able to deliver. But Self-Assurance is more than just self-confidence. Blessed with the theme of Self-Assurance, you have confidence not only in your abilities but in your judgment. When you look at the world, you know that your perspective is unique and distinct. And because no one sees exactly what you see, you know that no one can make your decisions for you. No one can tell you what to think. They can guide. They can suggest. But you alone have the authority to form conclusions, make decisions and act. This authority, this final accountability for the living of your life, does not intimidate you. On the contrary, it feels natural to you. No matter what the situation, you seem to know what the right decision is. This theme lends you an aura of certainty. Unlike many, you are not easily swayed by someone else's arguments, no matter how persuasive they may be. This Self-Assurance may be quiet or loud, depending on your other themes, but it is solid. It is strong. Like the keel of a ship, it withstands many different pressures and keeps you on your course.

Self-Assurance Action Items

- Life involves its share of disappointments and crises. Rely on your capacity to bounce back fast from setbacks. Help your friends and family who might not be as confident or certain as you are when they are going through tough times.

- Seek out internships in organizations that make you feel even *more* confident when you walk in the door. Your Self-Assurance talents, especially when combined with Command or Activator talents, can be extremely contagious. An organization that makes you feel confident and focused will make others feel confident and focused too.

- What are three ambitious goals you would like to achieve before completing your degree or certification? Go for the goals that may seem impractical and impossible to others but that are merely bold and exciting to you and — most importantly — achievable with some heroics.

- Get to know your professors and teaching assistants and what they expect from students in their classes. You are confident about your individual learning style, and by understanding their expectations, you can align your approaches with their goals for you. This will help you stay in control of your education.

- Once you set your sights on a goal, you are likely to stay with it until you achieve it. Seek out a mentor with strong Strategic, Deliberative or Futuristic talents. This person can look at the goals you commit to with a different perspective and help you decide if they are in your best interests.

- Help your friends set ambitious goals — they may not dream as big as you do. They might just need a push. Support them by believing in them. Your ability to take risks with certainty and your confidence can be contagious.

- Ask someone whose opinion you trust and respect to be your mentor. Everyone needs a mentor, and you might need one more than most. While you may think you are always right, nobody is right all the time. And second-guessing your decisions isn't something you do automatically. Good mentors will tell you when you're off track, and if you respect them and they respect you, you will listen to their guidance.

- How do you cope with mental stress? While confidence is the norm for you, when something shakes your sense of security, you feel it more intensely than others do — though you'll likely get through it faster than they will. When you're thrown off balance, look for campus resources and advisers that can help you get your mojo back.

- Join clubs that will stretch your talents and broaden your horizons. Dare to tackle the unfamiliar. You have the confidence to try new things. Invite some friends to take this journey with you.

- Consider a semester abroad. Your Self-Assurance talents will help you maneuver through a culture that is quite different from your own.

- Because of your Self-Assurance talents, you will probably be confident and comfortable in a variety of jobs and volunteer opportunities. Try out several different roles. Which ones seem most natural to you?

- Prominent or critical projects that might intimidate others seem to bring out your best. Research community initiatives online, and see what substantial projects are in the works. Find out how you can get involved in the initiatives that interest you most.

- Interview successful people in careers that align with your passions. Ask them what they find most rewarding about their work and what activities they participated in while they were in school. While you are likely confident in your own career path, hearing from others who found success can reinforce that you are on the right track.

Significance

You want to be very significant in the eyes of other people. In the truest sense of the word you want to be recognized. You want to be heard. You want to stand out. You want to be known. In particular, you want to be known and appreciated for the unique strengths you bring. You feel a need to be admired as credible, professional and successful. Likewise, you want to associate with others who are credible, professional and successful. And if they aren't, you will push them to achieve until they are. Or you will move on. An independent spirit, you want your work to be a way of life rather than a job, and in that work you want to be given free rein, the leeway to do things your way. Your yearnings feel intense to you, and you honor those yearnings. And so your life is filled with goals, achievements or qualifications that you crave. Whatever your focus — and each person is distinct — your Significance theme will keep pulling you upward, away from the mediocre toward the exceptional. It is the theme that keeps you reaching.

Significance Action Items

- Create a list of goals that will bring you satisfaction personally and academically. Then consider how your studies can help you reach those goals. Find people in your support system who can help you cultivate a reputation for excellence in the areas that matter to you most.

- Meet with your academic adviser to help you choose classes that allow independence, are relevant to your goals and desires, and in which you can be highly successful. You will thrive in courses where you have the autonomy to be exceptional.

- Take a leadership role in a study group, and choose to study with other ambitious classmates. As the leader, you will be at the forefront of the group and responsible for determining the best way to master the coursework.

- Identify the specific talents you will use to make an extraordinary contribution in your classes, campus clubs or internships. Create opportunities to stand out and show others the confidence you have in your strengths.

- Significant people do significant things. Imagine the legacy you want to leave. Picture yourself at retirement, looking back on a life that made the world a better place. What steps can you take now to make that future vision a reality?

- Leading crucial teams or significant projects brings out your best. You might be most motivated when the stakes are at their highest. Let others know that when the game is on the line, you want the ball. Your confidence to take big risks and carry the responsibility on your shoulders will comfort them.

- What makes you most proud of your friends and family members? Tell them. They will appreciate the positive recognition and attention, and you will feed your Significance talents through your association with them.

- The next time you're hanging out with friends, use five words to describe them, and ask them for five words that describe you. Knowing how others see you will help you maintain top-of-mind awareness of your talents and build your confidence.

- Are there alumni or professors you admire for their success? What do they have in common? Network with people whom you aspire to emulate. Ask them about the choices they made, what they find rewarding about the work they do and the risks they took to get where they are today. Ask them for practical advice and feedback about your own goals and strategies to determine if they think you're on the right path to success.

- You are independent and prioritize projects based on the level of influence they will have on the people around you. Look for clubs on campus where you can make the biggest impact. Define measurable goals that will show how you helped improve the organization.

- Make a list of goals, achievements and qualifications you crave, and post them where you will see them every day. Use this list to inspire yourself. What can you become involved in today that would be beneficial to have on your résumé?

- You will perform best when your performance is visible. Look for opportunities that put you on center stage. Stay away from roles that hide you behind the scenes.

- What can you do on campus that will help you stand out or become well-known? Consider running for student government, taking a leadership position in an extracurricular club, giving public speeches or volunteering to direct a community service project.

Strategic

The Strategic theme enables you to sort through the clutter and find the best route. It is not a skill that can be taught. It is a distinct way of thinking, a special perspective on the world at large. This perspective allows you to see patterns where others simply see complexity. Mindful of these patterns, you play out alternative scenarios, always asking, "What if this happened? Okay, well what if this happened?" This recurring question helps you see around the next corner. There you can evaluate accurately the potential obstacles. Guided by where you see each path leading, you start to make selections. You discard the paths that lead nowhere. You discard the paths that lead straight into resistance. You discard the paths that lead into a fog of confusion. You cull and make selections until you arrive at the chosen path — your strategy. Armed with your strategy, you strike forward. This is your Strategic theme at work: "What if?" Select. Strike.

Strategic Action Items

- Make full use of your Strategic talents by scheduling time to carefully think about a goal you want to achieve and the path you will take to reach it. Remember that time to contemplate is essential to strategic thinking.

- Initiate conversations about school logistics with other students. They, like you, need to figure out which classes to take and when, how to satisfy all the competing pressures of different assignments, and even the shortest routes between buildings. You will thrive in discussions like this, and you can make a huge difference by helping people who have less talent for strategizing.

- When you are looking for internships, play out different scenarios in your mind to help you decide which ones to explore further. List the various possible paths so you can give careful thought to each one.

- Picture yourself in a career you love. What are you doing? How did you get there? Working backward from your goal — and planning and refining your path — can inspire you and give you clarity about the future.

- Ask your roommates what goals they have achieved recently. How did they choose the route they took to achieve those goals? Think through and discuss with them the many options they had and the outcomes of their choices.

- Apply your natural "what if" thinking to help your friends and roommates arrive at their decisions. You naturally see alternatives more readily than others do. When your friends are stuck, share your insights and talk about the different options or paths they can take.

- You can figure out patterns and obstacles quickly, but when you're in class, you may struggle to explain what you see. What is so obvious to you might be invisible to others. Partner with someone with strong Communication or Individualization talents to help you articulate the steps you see so your classmates can understand what you're thinking.

- Seek out mentors with strong Achiever or Activator talents. While you can see the best path, they can make sure you get going and arrive at the destination.

- Partner with friends and classmates who have powerful Ideation talents to talk about all the alternative directions you see. These brainstorming sessions can help you become even better at anticipating and will inspire your strategic thinking.

- You have probably already thought of multiple paths you can take to receive your degree. To save money and reduce your overall student debt, meet with your academic adviser to see if there are any courses you do not need or that satisfy more than one area of your degree completion criteria.

- What are some real-world issues or needs that you can strategize with others about? Use your strategic thinking talents to be a powerful force for a good cause.

- Your ability to create new programs and generate multiple alternatives will be an asset to any organization you join. Before you interview for an internship or job, ask your professors and friends for feedback about how they see your talents best put to use.

- Is there an intramural sport or activity you would like to try? Consider joining athletic or other campus clubs that require a lot of strategy. Your talents for problem-solving and reaching the best conclusions could be quite useful in a competitive environment.

Woo

Woo stands for winning others over. You enjoy the challenge of meeting new people and getting them to like you. Strangers are rarely intimidating to you. On the contrary, strangers can be energizing. You are drawn to them. You want to learn their names, ask them questions and find some area of common interest so that you can strike up a conversation and build rapport. Some people shy away from starting up conversations because they worry about running out of things to say. You don't. Not only are you rarely at a loss for words; you actually enjoy initiating with strangers because you derive satisfaction from breaking the ice and making a connection. Once that connection is made, you are quite happy to wrap it up and move on. There are new people to meet, new rooms to work, new crowds to mingle in. In your world there are no strangers, only friends you haven't met yet — lots of them.

Woo Action Items

- Whatever you are doing, keep yourself involved with people. Study in places where there are other students around, like the common area in your residence hall or an off-campus coffee shop. Balance your academics with extracurricular activities so you have plenty of social time.

- Make a connection between what you are reading in your classes and people you have met. Because people fascinate you, when you associate them with your coursework, you are more likely to get involved in the reading and less likely to become bored — and you will better retain what you read.

- Try to meet professors before choosing your classes. Do they have open classroom discussions or group assignments? Ask other students about particular professors to make sure their style is the right fit for you. Your talents will flourish in classes where you can talk and work with other students.

- Introduce yourself to a lot of people in a wide variety of jobs. Broad exposure will give you a better idea of possible careers, and it could provide you with important professional and social connections for the future.

- You quicken the pulse of your surroundings. Recognize the power of your presence and of your Woo talents to open the door for an exchange of ideas in your classes or clubs. By simply starting conversations that engage others and bring talented people together, you can take performance up a notch — or several.

- Introduce some of the many people you know to your roommates and friends. They might enjoy getting to know a variety of other students as much as you do. And meeting new people might encourage your roommates and friends to work on their own social networks.

- You win friends and fans wherever you go, and that's a good thing. But remember that you've got lots of other talents and qualities that your Woo talents can outshine if you let them. Own all your talents and strengths, and be mindful about giving them the space and attention they deserve.

- When you need to develop contacts into long-lasting relationships, find friends with strong Empathy or Relator talents. They can help you adjust your typical pattern of meet, win over and move on to the next person so that you can invest the time and consideration that long-term friendships require.

- If you're looking for a part-time job, gravitate toward companies on or off campus that employ and serve students. Working at a business where other students

are your coworkers and customers will allow you
to meet more people you go to school with. Or use
your Woo talents to persuade a business to give you a
paid internship.

- What are your values? People with Woo are natural
  campaigners. Campaign for people and causes around
  your community that align with your values.

- Attend rush week activities to see if there's a
  fraternity or sorority you'd like to join. Whether or
  not you decide to pledge, rush is a great opportunity
  to network and meet lots of people who could become
  lifelong friends.

- Have you ever thought about running for an elected
  office? With exceptional Woo talents, you can
  quickly connect with people and make a positive first
  impression. Invite friends and classmates to help with
  your campaign.

- Consider becoming an orientation leader on campus.
  You will enjoy meeting newcomers and visitors and
  helping get people connected right away.

References

Busteed, B., & Seymour, S. (2015, September 23). Many college graduates not equipped for workplace success. Retrieved January 24, 2017, from http://www.gallup.com/businessjournal/185804/college-graduates-not-equipped-workplace-success.aspx?g_source=big%206&g_medium=search&g_campaign=tiles

Caspi, A., Harrington, H., Milne, B., Amell, J. W., Theodore, R. F., & Moffitt, T. E. (2003). Children's behavioral styles at age 3 are linked to their adult personality traits at age 26. *Journal of Personality*, 71(4), 495-514.

Clifton, D. O., Anderson, E., & Schreiner, L. A. (2006). *StrengthsQuest: Discover and develop your strengths in academics, career, and beyond.* Washington, D.C.: Gallup Organization.

Clifton, D. O., & Harter, J. K. (2003). Investing in Strengths. In K. S. Cameron, J. E. Dutton, & R. E. Quinn (Eds.), *Positive organizational scholarship: foundations of a new discipline* (pp. 111-121). San Francisco, CA: Berrett-Koehler.

Csikszentmihalyi, M. (1990). *Flow: the psychology of optimal experience.* New York: Harper & Row.

Gallup. (n.d.). Aiming higher education at great jobs and great lives. Retrieved January 24, 2017, from http://www.gallup.com/services/170939/higher-education.aspx

Gallup. (n.d.). Discover your strengths: CliftonStrengths. Retrieved January 24, 2017, from http://www.gallup.com/products/170957/clifton-strengthsfinder.aspx

Gallup. (n.d.). Strengths: History. Retrieved January 24, 2017, from http://strengths.gallup.com/110443/History.aspx

Gallup, Purdue University, & Lumina. (2014). *Great jobs, great lives: The 2014 Gallup-Purdue Index report.* Omaha, NE: Gallup.

Harter, J., & Arora, R. (2008, June 5). Social time crucial to daily emotional wellbeing in U.S. Retrieved January 24, 2017, from http://www.gallup.com/poll/107692/social-time-crucial-daily-emotional-wellbeing.aspx

History of NHRRF: The Nebraska Human Resources Research Foundation. (n.d.). Retrieved January 24, 2017, from http://alec.unl.edu/nhri/history-nhrrf

Irwin-Gish, S. (2015, June 5). Clifton Foundation, Gallup donate $30M to UNL CBA for Don Clifton Strengths Institute. Retrieved January 24, 2017, from http://newsroom.unl.edu/releases/2015/06/05/Clifton+Foundation,+Gallup+donate+$30M+to+UNL+CBA+for+Don+Clifton+Strengths+Institute

Liesveld, R., Miller, J. A., & Robison, J. (2005). *Teach with your strengths: how great teachers inspire their students.* New York: Gallup Press.

Rath, T. (2007). *StrengthsFinder 2.0.* New York: Gallup Press.

Rath, T., & Conchie, B. (2008). *Strengths based leadership: great leaders, teams, and why people follow.* New York: Gallup Press.

Rath, T., & Harter, J. (2010). *Wellbeing: the five essential elements.* New York: Gallup Press.

Rath, T., & Harter, J. (2010, July 22). Your career wellbeing and your identity. Retrieved January 24, 2017, from http://www.gallup.com/businessjournal/127034/career-wellbeing-identity.aspx

Rath, T., & Harter, J. (2010, August 19). Your friends and your social wellbeing. Retrieved January 24, 2017, from http://www.gallup.com/businessjournal/127043/friends-social-wellbeing.aspx

Saad, L. (2014, August 29). The "40-hour" workweek is actually longer — by seven hours. Retrieved January 24, 2017, from http://www.gallup.com/poll/175286/hour-workweek-actually-longer-seven-hours.aspx

Smith, B., & Rutigliano, T. (2003). *Discover your sales strengths: how the world's greatest salespeople develop winning careers.* New York: Warner Books.

The History of CliftonStrengths

*"What would happen if we studied what was **right** with people?"*
— Dr. Don Clifton (1924–2003)

This simple question, posed six decades ago by Don Clifton, launched the global strengths movement.

The question was particularly personal for Don.

During World War II, Clifton put his mathematics skills to the test as an Army Air Force navigator flying on B-24s. While flying over the Azores in bad weather, his flight went off course. Don had a hunch about how to correct it. But when he did the math, he realized his intuition was wrong. He learned to trust science over personal intuition.

Don received the Distinguished Flying Cross for heroism during his 25 successful bombing sorties. But when he returned home from WWII, he had seen enough war and destruction. He wanted to spend the rest of his life doing good for humankind. This led to his intense interest in studying human development in a different way — studying what was *right* with people.

"In my graduate study in psychology, it became evident to me that psychologists had historically studied what was wrong with people rather than what worked," Don said. "I realized then that too often, people were being characterized by their problems and weaknesses rather than their talents. That realization led me to the necessity for studying successful people. The only way to learn to identify the differences in any professions is to study the successful performers."

In 1949, Clifton and his colleagues started the Nebraska Human Resources Research Foundation at the University of Nebraska. The foundation served as a community service for students and as a laboratory for graduate students to practice strengths-based psychology. Don and his students and colleagues discovered that successful students — those who persisted to graduation — had notably different character traits than less successful ones.

These early discoveries about successful people stirred other hypotheses. Don and his colleagues began to study the most successful school counselors, teachers, salespeople and managers. Don discovered that successful people in specific roles shared certain traits. He defined those tendencies as "naturally recurring patterns of thought, feeling or behavior that can be productively applied."

Don wanted to identify universal but practical traits that were predictive of high-performance outcomes. And he wanted to identify tendencies that were unique to each individual but that could be developed into strengths with practice. The purpose of this work was to bring focus to conversations so people could better understand not just who they are — but what they could become.

Dr. Clifton developed hundreds of predictive instruments that identified top performers for specific jobs within an organization's unique culture. These scientifically validated instruments found the best talent fit for the right position in a specific company.

But there was something missing.

The ability to identify great talent for an organization was not always helpful to individuals. So, in the mid-1990s, Clifton developed an assessment that identified specific traits and a framework for developing those traits for the benefit of individuals. He labeled those traits "strengths."

Along his journey to create what would become the CliftonStrengths assessment, Don met with many academics and fellow researchers. Perhaps the most significant connection was with Harvard psychology professor Phil Stone. Dr. Stone was deemed a child prodigy, entering the University of Chicago at age 15 and earning two Ph.D.s by age 23. He taught psychology at Harvard for 39 years. Along with his passion for social sciences, Dr. Stone was an advocate for a newly discovered technology called "the internet."

Dr. Stone's two recommendations for Dr. Clifton were to build the assessment for the coming digital age and to use a modified ipsative scoring algorithm, rather than the customary normative scoring, as in the Likert scale (1-5) or multiple choice. Ipsative scoring asks a respondent to choose between two socially desirable outcomes. It is based on the assumption that individuals are often presented with multiple positive alternatives in real-life situations — for example, "I organize" and "I analyze." Ipsative measurement is particularly useful in identifying intrapersonal characteristics — it reduces social desirability bias, or "gaming," that can happen with many normative measurements.

One of the first uses of what was to become the CliftonStrengths assessment was when Harvard psychology students took the assessment and provided feedback on the themes and theme descriptors.

In 1997, Clifton and Stone developed a workbook called "Corner of the Sky," which Stone used in his psychology classes at Harvard. This was the beginning of the impact of strengths on college campuses and the dawn of the positive psychology movement.

On the West Coast, UCLA social scientist Dr. Edward "Chip" Anderson took an interest in Don's work. In 1998, Clifton and Anderson developed "Soaring With Your Strengths," a course supplement for UCLA students. This early draft later became the foundation for the groundbreaking book *StrengthsQuest: Discover and Develop Your Strengths in Academics, Career, and Beyond.*

Another critical member of Don's research and development team was Gallup IT specialist Jon Conradt. Jon worked closely with Don to develop the assessment's digital platform and algorithmic scoring. Most of the original code remains as the backbone of CliftonStrengths technology today.

Don distilled all of these research findings into the original 34 strengths themes that became StrengthsFinder and later CliftonStrengths.

Clifton's work has inspired books read by millions around the world, including *Soar With Your Strengths*, which Don coauthored with Paula Nelson; *Strengths Based Leadership*, by Tom Rath and Barry Conchie; *How Full Is Your Bucket?*, by Don and Tom Rath; *Now, Discover Your Strengths*, which Don coauthored with Marcus Buckingham; *CliftonStrengths for Students*, by Tom Matson; and one of the bestselling business books of all time, *StrengthsFinder 2.0*, by Tom Rath.

Near the end of his life, Don was honored with a Presidential Commendation by the American Psychological Association as the Father of Strengths-Based Psychology.

Dr. Clifton's mission upon returning from World War II was to make a significant contribution to human development. As of this writing, over 21 million people have discovered their CliftonStrengths.

Don changed the world.

About Gallup

Gallup is a global analytics, advisory and learning firm that helps leaders solve their organizations' biggest problems.

Gallup knows more about the will of employees, customers, students and citizens than any other organization in the world. We offer solutions, transformations and services in many areas, including:

- Culture change
- Leadership development
- Manager development
- Strengths-based coaching and culture
- Strategies for organic growth
- "Boss-to-coach" software tools
- Attracting and recruiting star team members
- Succession planning
- Performance management system and ratings
- Refining performance metrics
- Reducing defects and safety risks
- Evaluating internal programs

- Employee engagement and experience
- Predictive hiring assessments
- Retention forecasting
- Creating agile teams
- Improving the customer experience (B2B)
- Diversity and inclusion
- Wellbeing initiatives

To learn more, please contact Gallup at **https://www.gallup.com/contact.**

Acknowledgements

To Don Clifton, Father of Strengths Psychology, whose insights inspired every word of this book, every other strengths book published by Gallup and the fast-growing global strengths movement.

To Tom Matson for his deep insights into strengths, masterful storytelling and reporting, and for bringing Don's decades of work to life in every page of this book.

To Jennifer Robison, whose exceptional editing and writing talent and rare ability to weave a compelling narrative were essential to the development of this book.

To the thousands of educators who change the lives of students daily by helping them align their strengths to relationships, academics, careers and life. In particular, thanks to Dr. Mike Finnegan, Grant Anderson and Kristin Brunkow for modeling best practice and mentorship and for living Don's legacy every day.

To Jim Clifton and Jon Clifton for their passion to continue their father's and grandfather's vision for thousands of colleges and universities, faculty, staff and students around the world. Both of them poured themselves into this book to make sure it honored Don's vision and were its biggest champions.

To Geoff Brewer for his constant support, guidance and strategic lens and to Seth Schuchman for his leadership, belief and vision for this book. Plus, to the rest of the Gallup Press team who made every word and detail shine: Kelly Henry, Leigh Gobber, Becky McCarville, Jessica Kennedy, Sam Allemang, Tim Dean and Jenni Gardner.

To Dr. Jim Harter and Jim Asplund for their partnership, incredible expertise and ability to make the research move from numbers to change lives.

To Allyson Negrete for pouring herself into creating perfect words that created a call to strengths in action that leads to a thriving life.

To Katie Lyon for her continued leadership and support for strengths in education.

To the many Gallup associates who added their support, thought leadership and expertise: Paul Allen, Brandon Busteed, Benjamin Erikson-Farr, Kristin Gregory, Trista Kunce, Tom Melanson, Cara Meyer, Emily Meyer, Matt Mosser, Mark Pogue, Connie Rath, Tom Rath, Phil Ruhlman, Chris Sheehan, Lindsey Spehn, Ben Wigert and Anna Zelaya.

Gallup Press exists to educate and inform the people who govern, manage, teach and lead the world's 7 billion citizens. Each book meets Gallup's requirements of integrity, trust and independence and is based on Gallup-approved science and research.

This packet contains:

Your unique access code*
to take the CliftonStrengths®
assessment.

* This access code is valid for one use only.
  Do not buy this book if this packet has
  been opened.

Your unique access code* to take the
CliftonStrengths® assessment is:

X2J8P4N8R9Y6G2

To redeem your code, visit:

press.gallup.com/code/students

*This access code is valid for one use only.

This packet contains:

Your unique access code*
to take the CliftonStrengths®
assessment.

* This access code is valid for one use only.
  Do not buy this book if this packet has
  been opened.